In Tables of Stone

Shawn Boonstra

with Clifford Goldstein

and Pacific Press Publishing Association

Book Design and Layout by Fred Knopper
Cover Illustration by Palmer Halvorson
Edited by Judy Knopper
Proofread by Ashley Wagner
Text Typeset: 12 pt. ITC New Baskerville

Additional copies of this book and many
other spiritual resources are available by
calling toll free 1-888-664-5573 or visiting
www.itiswritten.com

Printed in the United States of America
by Pacific Press Publishing Association
Nampa, Idaho / Oshawa, Ontario, Canada
www.pacificpress.com

ISBN 13: 978-0-8163-2295-4
ISBN 10: 0-8163-2295-3

Contents

CHAPTER ONE

For YOUR GOOD

The day hadn't started very well for ten-year-old Natascha Kampusch of Vienna, Austria. For starters her parents had just gone through a nasty divorce, which was pretty hard on her and her siblings. To make matters worse, she had gotten in a fight with her mother soon after getting up. Little did the young red-haired girl know just how bad the day was going to get. In fact, that morning was the beginning of an eight-year nightmare for her and her family.

On the morning of March 2, 1986, Natascha was on her way to school. It was cool outside, with some snow on the ground. Along the way a white minivan with darkened windows approached her. Before she knew it, she had been grabbed, forcibly thrown into the van, and whisked away.

Natascha's abduction led to a massive nationwide search, perhaps the greatest in Austria's history. Just about every white minivan in the nation was checked—about seven hundred of them. Riverbeds and gravel pits all across the country, and even over the border into Hungary, were searched carefully for clues to her disappearance. Every possible lead was followed, and yet, when it was all over, no one discovered what had happened to her. She simply disappeared, and over time many people just assumed that the unfortunate child was dead.

Among those questioned by the police was a thirty-eight-year-old communications technician named Wolfgang Priklopil. He was the owner of a white van that fit the description of the one seen in Natascha's abduction. But Wolfgang had a pretty good alibi, and the police let him go. It's unfortunate they didn't look a lot closer at Mr. Priklopil. As the world now knows, he was the one who had taken the child, holding her in a makeshift prison in the basement of his small house in a Vienna suburb. Her cell was about ten by six by five feet at the bottom of a cement staircase, and sealed with an electronically operated latch. It was in this cramped cell that little Natascha Kampusch was to spend most of the next eight years of her life.

All sorts of grisly stories have been circulating about what Natascha had to endure during her eight-year imprisonment. There is no question that some abuse occurred, even though clear details still have not emerged. We do know, however, that a strange relationship developed between Natascha and her captor during the time of her captivity. Priklopil actually brought her books, and continued her education right there in the cell. He became a father figure to her, teaching her geography and history, and reading her stories. She later said that, "He brought me books to read, and I asked him totally normal childhood questions about foreign countries, and animals."

All the while that Priklopil was educating his young prisoner, he tried to destroy her hopes of being rescued. "He told me," she said, that "he was continually calling my parents. They could have me back if they were ready to pay him ten million schillings. But he told me they never picked up the telephone, because I was obviously not important to them." Over time he let her upstairs where they ate together, watched TV, and where she even cleaned his house. He had warned her over and over that he would "grill to the bone" anyone who entered the house. He also told her that he slept with grenades under his pillow, and that the house was wired with explosives that would blow her up should she try to escape.

After a number of years, he took her on small outings, warning her that if she said anything to anyone he would kill that person. One time he actually took her on a ski trip to a nearby ski resort. On the way there they were stopped by the police for a routine check; yet, out of fear, the girl didn't utter a single word. She reported, however, that from the first day of her captivity all she ever thought about was escape; but she was afraid of what might happen if she didn't make it. He had told her that he was heavily armed and would kill them both if she tried anything.

Meanwhile, neighbors had seen them drive off a few times together. Josef Jantschek, who lived nearby, said, "I saw the young lady in the garden quite often over the past year. They also drove off together in his car, and every time she waved at us in a friendly way." He added, "We could not have known that it was the kidnapped Natascha Kampusch. When I asked him whether she was his new girlfriend, he only said, 'I have borrowed her from a work colleague to do some work for me.'"

Then, on August 23, 2006, Natascha finally did what she had been dreaming about for eight long years. She was in his garden, vacuuming his BMW, when he got a cellphone call. Because of the noise of the vacuum, he walked away. After a few moments of hesitation, the eighteen-year-old woman made a run for it. She ran through gardens, across lawns, jumped over fences, and ran across streets. She covered about six hundred yards, screaming to anyone she saw to please call the police. Incredibly, most people didn't pay any attention to her.

After about five minutes of running, she knocked on the window of a house. A seventy-one-year-old woman opened it and looked out. When she did, Natascha yelled, "I am Natascha Kampusch!"

The woman called the police, and within an hour Natascha was safely at the police station. Wolfgang Priklopil, no doubt knowing that it was all over, and that he faced the rest of his life in prison, committed suicide by throwing himself in front of a commuter train a few hours after her escape.

I find this story absolutely fascinating, because of one simple fact. There was absolute, universal moral condemnation of what Mr. Priklopil did to Natascha Kampusch. Everyone, everywhere, found his actions absolutely horrifying. There was no moral wavering, no equivocating, no talk of competing values, or "not judging" Mr. Priklopil's actions by our own moral standards when he might have been living by a different moral code. Instinctively everyone knew it was wrong.

I find that very interesting, because we live in a time of rampant and unrestrained moral relativism. There's the idea that different people have different concepts of right and wrong, and that we should all learn to live with it. It's been said that people in one culture, or one society, shouldn't judge people living in another culture, because we don't have that right—no matter how strange or even objectionable their actions might appear to be.

This is the main and overarching view of what has been called postmodernism. To understand what postmodernism is, we need to understand modernism, or the modern era. Quite simply, the modern era is the era of science, of Isaac Newton, of reason and experiment. The modern era began when people stopped blaming their crop failures on spells cast by witches, and blamed poor agricultural practices instead. The modern era began when outbreaks of pestilence were no longer blamed on Jews poisoning the wells, but on germs and improper hygiene. The modern age is when humans replaced superstitions with chemistry, with physics, and mathematical formulas and laws, an age that basically claims that all reality can be objectively explained through principles of science and mathematics.

When a childhood friend of mine got his first telescope, he was sure that he was going to be an astronomer. He had visions of sitting on Mt. Palomar with a giant fifty-foot long telescope, scanning the wonders of the cosmos. As he looked into astronomy a little more, he discovered that it was mostly math, numbers, and formulas, and he hated those things. Today, I think he's a plumber.

One of the most humorous examples of this kind of thinking comes from the British political writer Jeremy Bentham, who died in 1832. Bentham attempted to take all aspects of human life and break it down into science and math. He once proposed marriage to a young lady in a letter where, using mathematical formulas, he worked out why this woman should marry him. I don't know the math itself, but I suppose he calculated their ages, their wealth, and the expected number of years they would live together, etc. Needless to say, however good his calculations were mathematically, they weren't exactly adequate to win her heart, and she turned him down. Years later he sent another letter, this time with revised calculations to reflect their changed circumstances, again hoping to win her hand in marriage. I don't have to tell you what her answer was.

Here's the point. However good and effective reason, science, and math are for creating computers, or for building rockets, they can't explain every aspect of human life. There's simply more to a human being than what science or math can account for. And so, many people have moved away from this hardcore attempt at scientific and mathematical objectivity of the modern era to the opposite extreme. Hence, we are now in the postmodern era, where the notion of objective truths is rejected, and replaced by more subjective things like emotions, culture, and personal preference.

There's just one overwhelming problem. In this view there is no real truth at all. Truth is relative, contingent, changing; it depends upon culture, education, and upbringing, especially in the area of morals. Different groups have different moral standards, and so no one has the right to judge the moral standards of one culture by their own moral standards. After all, who is to say that one person's moral culture is better than another's. So the popular thinking is that we shouldn't pass judgment on what others do.

I'm all for tolerance and understanding, but it kind of falls apart when you follow it through to its logical conclusion. Let's go back to the story of Natascha Kampusch for just a moment. If moral values are relative, then why was everyone so angry at what her captor did? Isn't that just his style of living, his own set of moral standards?

Suppose we discovered a new culture somewhere in the South Pacific where it is common for men to kidnap children from other families and hold them captive for years. Would you just shrug your shoulders and say, "Well, we might not like it, but that's their culture. Who are we to say that it's wrong"? We might be tempted to say that about the South Pacific, but why do we then reject it in the case of Wolfgang Priklopil?

Let me give you another real life example. A lot of horror stories have been coming out of Iraq in recent years, but there's one that I find especially haunting. In addition to ceaseless bombings, the Iraqi nation has been plagued by kidnappings. People, often children, are snatched away, and the family gets them back only if they pay a ransom. As bad as that is, it gets worse. In some cases when a female kidnap victim is returned, a male member of the family, the father, or maybe a brother, feels duty bound to kill the girl. They kill an innocent victim, because they believe she might have been violated while in captivity, and in order to protect the family's honor she has to be put to death.

Tell me, can you really say, "Well, who are we to judge? After all, it's their culture, so why should we pass judgment on someone killing his own sister?" It's just not possible to do that. But if this idea of cultural relativism is right, then you have no choice but to accept that behavior. By our standards it's horrible, but by other standards it's the only honorable thing to do. So how can we deem those actions to be wrong?

When you get right to the bottom line, moral relativism simply does not work. Just because something is deemed right in a culture doesn't make it any more right than if just one person believes it is right. The Nazis were fanatically convinced that they were right, yet all the conviction in the world won't turn a death camp into something good. There are certain things we know are wrong, regardless of culture or personal preferences.

An atheist was debating a Christian on this whole question of moral values. The atheist was insisting that morals are purely subjective, and purely personal. "One set of values," he said, "is just as good as another." The Christian thought about it and responded: "Well, sir, in some societies people are taught to love their neighbor, and in other societies they are taught to eat them. Which do you think is better?"

When God condemned the practices of pagan nations—things like child sacrifice and religious prostitution—can you really see Moses saying, "Come on, Lord, don't judge those people by Your standards, they're just following their own traditions." Of course not. In fact, Moses said this to the children of Israel after they had sinned against the Lord:

"You shall not at all do as we are doing here today—every man doing whatever is right in his own eyes—" (Deuteronomy 12:8)

In another place, the Bible says, "In those days there was no king in Israel; everyone did what was right in his own eyes" (Judges 21:25). And Proverbs says, "The way of a fool is right in his own eyes..." (Proverbs 12:15).

Do you see it? Doing what you think is right can make about as much sense as someone saying, "I don't care what the compass tells me, I think north is in the opposite direction."

There's just no question about it. There really are absolute moral values, absolute moral truths, and that's because God is a God of morality. Just as He created the universe with physical laws, He also created it with moral laws. That's why we instinctively know that certain things are just flat-out wrong, like what Wolfgang Priklopil did to Natascha Kampusch.

There *is* right and wrong, good and evil, and the good news in all this is that God has not left us in the dark to figure it out. He has given us a standard, an absolute standard, of right and wrong. It's called the Ten Commandments, God's moral law. Yes, the famous Ten Commandments engraved in stone: written in something permanent.

Jesus Himself was very clear on the importance of keeping those Ten Commandments. Someone came to Him and said:

"... Good Teacher, what shall I do that I may inherit eternal life?" (Mark 10:17)

And Jesus answered like this:

"You know the commandments: 'Do not commit adultery,' 'Do not murder,' 'Do not steal,' 'Do not bear false witness,' 'Do not defraud,' 'Honor your father and your mother.'" (Mark 10:19)

To be honest, that doesn't sound like God changed His mind about right and wrong, does it? Years later, Paul said:

Circumcision is nothing and uncircumcision is nothing, but keeping the commandments of God is what matters. (1 Corinthians 7:19)

Even later, John the Revelator said:

Here is the patience of the saints; here are those who keep the commandments of God and the faith of Jesus. (Revelation 14:12)

There's a reason those laws were written in stone by the finger of God Himself. It's because He meant them to last forever.

I know that people will say, "The Ten Commandments are so restrictive, so limiting of my freedom to do what I want!" But if you think about it, you can't really say that. Just ask the nineteen-year-old girl I know of who, through violation of one of the Ten Commandments, contracted HIV, and is now on the way to full blown AIDS. Ask her how restricting she thinks the Ten

Commandments are. Or ask the eight-year-old boy whose life fell apart after his father left his mother, and ran away with the office secretary. Ask him how restricting, how awful, he thinks the Ten Commandments are. And if you could, ask any of the thousands of people murdered in America each year how restricting they think the Ten Commandments to be. Ask the people rotting in jail for theft if they think the Ten Commandments are too restrictive. I'm willing to bet that most of these people only wish they had followed God's loving moral guidelines.

The Ten Commandments are really not restrictive at all. To say that, is like telling me I'm restrictive of my two daughters because I don't want them playing in the street with traffic, or putting their hands on a hot stove, or experimenting with cocaine, or PCP, or heroin when they get older. It's not restrictive; it's just common sense.

For the same reason God has given our world a code of good moral conduct, because He knows for sure what's best for us. He gave it to us because He wants us to avoid the suffering that's caused by breaking His law.

My goal in this book is for you to be able to see the love of God in those tables of stone, to see a much better plan for a much better life. I want you to see for yourself the reality of these words when the Lord told His people that He wanted them "to keep the commandments of the LORD and His statutes which I command you today for your good" (Deuteronomy 10:13).

Did you notice the last part? God says it's "for your good." He didn't just dream up a bunch of rules to make your life miserable, or to ruin your fun. In fact, Jesus said that He came to give us a more abundant life. It's all for our good.

Just try to imagine how much better our world would be if everyone were living according to those ten simple commandments. No murder, no theft, no adultery, no lying. I think that would be a pretty nice place to live. Of course, I know you can't change the whole world; but what about changing yourself? Wouldn't that be a pretty good start?

I know we've all broken God's law. We're all sinners, and we all face the immediate, and sometimes terrible, consequences of having broken God's moral principles. The horrible results of human rebellion are everywhere, and the sad thing is our violation of the law doesn't just hurt ourselves. It usually means someone else gets hurt, too: just ask Natascha Kampusch.

The good news is that Jesus died for those who have broken God's law. He paid the penalty for our transgressions, and as a result we can be forgiven and cleansed of our sin. The Bible says:

If we confess our sins, He is faithful and just to forgive us our sins and to cleanse us from all unrighteousness. (1 John 1:9)

That's really good news, but the news gets even better. The Bible also says He will make us new creatures.

Therefore, if anyone is in Christ, he is a new creation; old things have passed away; behold, all things have become new. (2 Corinthians 5:17)

We get new tendencies, and new spiritual desires. That means that right now, through His power, you can start living in harmony with His moral law, and spare yourself so much of the suffering that inevitably comes from breaking it. I don't know about you, but that sounds like a pretty good deal to me.

CHAPTER TWO

Einstein's BRAIN

Albert Einstein continues to hold an incredible fascination for us. Every year scholarly books are written about his theories, professional conferences are held to discuss his achievements, and new technical works are presented that debate the unanswered questions Einstein raised about the nature of time and space.

Not only has Einstein enjoyed considerable popularity in scientific circles, but he's also been a subject of the popular media as well.

In 2005 Jean-Claude Carrier wrote a novel called *Einstein S'il Vous Plait* (or in English, *Please, Mr. Einstein*). Walter Matthau played the role of Einstein in the film *I.Q,* Alan Lightman wrote a novel called *Einstein's Dreams,* and comedian Steve Martin did an entire play about Einstein. He was the subject of Philip Glass's 1976 opera, *Einstein on the Beach,* and an Australian filmmaker named Yahoo Serious (no kidding, that's his real name) made a movie called *Young Einstein.*

If you type in "Albert Einstein" on Amazon.com, you'll discover scores of titles on this man, everything from *Einstein's Universe; Relativity Made Plain,* to a book called, *365 Days of Baby Einstein.*

Every year *TIME* magazine has its annual Man of the Year award. But in 1999 it did something unusual; it named Albert Einstein Man of the Century. I didn't really need to tell you all that in order for you to know that "Einstein" is basically a household word.

But few people know much about him, except for the fact that he came up with $E=mc^2$. If you start digging, you will find all sorts of fascinating stories about his life, especially his early years. For example, few people realize that Einstein was a very late talker. Even at nine years of age he wasn't fluent in his native German, and his parents feared he might be mentally deficient. He wasn't a particularly good student either, and according to Einstein biographer Ronald W. Clark, when his father asked Albert's schoolmaster what profession his son should pursue the schoolmaster replied, "Well, it doesn't matter; he'll never make a success of anything." Imagine that: Albert Einstein predicted to be a failure.

In 1895 at the age of sixteen, Albert Einstein took the entrance examination for the Swiss Federal Institute of Technology. He passed with flying colors, right? Wrong. He was a miserable failure: he flunked! But within ten years, as a "not-especially-good" school teacher who was serving as a minor civil servant in a patent office in Berne, Switzerland, Einstein wrote four papers on physics that literally changed the way we look at the universe. I somehow doubt that back then anybody could have grasped just how profoundly Einstein was about to impact the world.

In fact, in 1921 a young student approached Einstein, by then already world-renowned, and said he believed that from Einstein's formula, $E=mc^2$ you could split the atom and create a nuclear weapon. Einstein just brushed him off, told the young man it was foolishness, and that he didn't want to talk about it anymore. But you and I know that about twenty-four years later, nuclear weapons were invented, based on Einstein's formula, and for better or for worse, we entered the nuclear age.

I'm not going to pretend to be able to explain all of Einstein's theories in this short chapter, but let's take a stab at the basics. Let's say we have a pair of twins, Hans and Louie. Hans loves planes and rockets, and all his life he wanted to be an astronaut. But Louie is different because he doesn't like heights. He doesn't even like looking out a second story window. The boys grow up, Hans becomes an astronaut, and Louie becomes an accountant.

When both turn twenty, Hans takes off on a thirty-year mission in a rocket that can travel near the speed of light. That is 180,000 miles per second, which means that at the speed of light you could go around the world seven times in one second. The brothers say good-bye, and Louie watches Hans blast off in his rocket. Years pass, Louie gets married, has children, gets grey hair, wrinkles, a little arthritis in the knee, and a bit of a beer belly. After thirty years, Hans returns from space. Louie runs out to meet him, but can't believe what he sees. Louie is fifty years old, but Hans doesn't look any older than the day he left. In fact, according to Han's calendar, he was gone only two years.

How could that be? I can't explain how, other than Einstein taught that when you get close to the speed of light, time slows down. So what was thirty years for Louie felt like only two years for Hans. That may be hard to wrap your mind around, but that's the way a lot of people interpret the theory of relativity. That theory has given us explanations for the universe that filled in some of the gaps in Newton's discovery of the laws of gravity. Try to picture this scene. Young Einstein is in the midst of looking at other peoples' patents for things like mouse traps and dog collars, and while he's working he figures out that the faster you move the slower time goes. And, according to the math, he appears to be right! No wonder people are obsessed with his brain.

And what a brain it was. A few years after the theory of relativity, Einstein came up with another theory even more complicated. The only problem was that this new theory needed experimental verification, and because of World War I it was going to be a few years before it could be done. In the meantime, someone asked Einstein, "Suppose the experiment proves your theory wrong?" Einstein said, "So much worse for the experiment. The theory's right." It *was* right, and our understanding of the world has never been the same since.

Einstein's story has a flip side, too. One woman tells the story of Einstein at a fancy black-tie party given in his honor. All the guests were wearing tuxedos, and gowns: a very formal affair. The woman saw Einstein sitting there in his tuxedo with crossed legs, and she noticed something strange: Einstein wasn't wearing any socks. On another occasion, a person who lived in the same town as Einstein said that someone wearing a hat and sunglasses approached him on the street and asked directions to a house. That wouldn't be strange, except for the fact that the house was Einstein's and the person asking was Einstein. In spite of all his genius, he couldn't find his own home!

The fascination with Einstein's brain took a ghoulish twist soon after he died. The doctor who did the autopsy actually stole Einstein's brain, supposedly for medical research. He never did do any real research on it however, and allegedly gave out pieces over the next thirty years to friends and other researchers.

Toward the end of his life, the doctor, perhaps feeling guilty, got in touch with Einstein's closest relative, a granddaughter living in California, and decided to return what was left of the brain to her. A journalist named Michael Paterniti heard about it and offered to drive the doctor, who was living on the East Coast, all the way to California. Paterniti later wrote a book called *Driving Mr. Albert,* all about this cross-country trip with the remains of Albert Einstein's brain sloshing around in a Tupperware container filled with formaldehyde in the trunk of a Buick Skylark.

But the most interesting part of this story is at that point when Paterniti was sitting in the car with Einstein's granddaughter in front of her apartment building. They opened the Tupperware container, and she picked up a few of the pieces of the brain. Then, with the greatest brain of the modern era in her hand, she said something very interesting: "So this is what the fuss is all about?"

Here they were, literally holding in their hands the organ where some of the most profound and world changing ideas in history were formed. One has to ask, could Einstein, with all his genius, all of his ideas and passions, really be confined to this simple brain matter, those ridges and crevices of fibers and neurons sitting in their hands? Is that really what all the fuss was about? In the end, was Albert Einstein nothing but a bit of physical tissue, a body of flesh and bones, a lump of gray matter, and nothing more?

Is that, in fact, what we all are: purely physical beings, existing only because of purely physical laws that produce emotions, ideas, creativity, and art the way the stomach produces hydrochloric acid? Are we just a physical phenomenon: the motion of atoms, the synthesis of proteins, and the flow of blood and hormones? Is that all Albert Einstein's genius was? Could you find the secret of Einstein's genius within the physical structure of his brain?

In order to answer that question, you must first answer the question of human origin. If we are simply the chance product of physical forces alone, as so many scientists and philosophers have told us, then I guess that's all we could be: just physical beings living in a physical world, with nothing transcendent above or beyond us. And if modern science is right, I'm afraid that's the conclusion we have to come to.

Just think about what your high school textbooks told you about the origin of human life. Billions of years ago there was a massive explosion, and hot globules of matter congregated all over the universe. Some of them, including that which made our earth, cooled down and condensed. Over time warm pools of water formed. In them simple proteins and amino acids mysteriously emerged, and in time they somehow turned into primitive life. Over millions and millions of years, this primitive life form evolved through a vicious battle of survival of the fittest to eventually become, among other things, Einstein's brain.

That kind of thinking leaves one feeling just a little empty. I like how sociologist Peter Berger phrased it: "There is really nothing very funny about finding oneself stranded, alone, in a remote corner of a universe bereft of human meaning—nor about the idea that this fate is the outcome of the mindless massacre that Darwin, rather euphemistically, called natural selection." And I've got to agree; it's not funny at all.

French biologist and atheist Jacques Monod wrote: "The ancient covenant is in pieces; man knows at last that he is alone in the universe's unfeeling immensity, out of which he emerged only by chance. His destiny is nowhere spelled out, nor is his duty. The kingdom above or the darkness below; it is for him to choose."

I'm not quite sure just where Mr. Monod thinks he's going to find a "kingdom above" in a godless universe where we all emerged by chance. But setting that aside, if I accepted his idea that we are indeed alone in the universe, I think I'd start to feel a little pessimistic, too.

But I don't accept that view, not at all. I have a totally different view of human origin. I believe that we're here because a loving Creator, the God revealed in the pages of the Bible, created us and breathed into us what the Bible calls "… the breath of life …" (Genesis 2:7). I believe we're here not because "In the beginning, cold, mindless, uncaring forces created the heavens and the earth," but because "In the beginning God created the heavens and the earth" (Genesis 1:1).

I believe that we're here, not because of evolution, or natural selection, or genetic mutation, but because God said in Genesis, chapter one:

"Let Us make man in Our image, according to Our likeness; let them have dominion over the fish of the sea, over the birds of the air, and over

the cattle, over all the earth and over every creeping thing that creeps on the earth." So God created man in His own *image; in the image of God He created him; male and female He created them. Then God blessed them, and God said to them, "Be fruitful and multiply; fill the earth and subdue it; have dominion over the fish of the sea, over the birds of the air, and over every living thing that moves on the earth."* (*Genesis 1:26-28*)

That's the only thing that really makes sense. It gives us the meaning in life that we all crave so badly. There is a reason for our existence; somebody *wanted* us here. And because that someone is our Creator, I worship Him.

Directly tied in with this concept of a God who created us, is the question of morality. If we accept the atheistic view of our origins, then we have to admit that ideas like good and evil or right and wrong, are nothing but human concoctions; the products of culture only. And if you accept that morality is something invented by human beings, then you run into a big problem. If one culture says it's okay to throw young virgins into an active volcano in order to appease the gods of the underworld, then who is allowed to say that it's wrong? By what authority can they possibly critique that behavior? What gives one culture the right to judge the moral codes and traditions of another culture, especially if we all came into existence by random chance? What basis do you have for a common morality? It would seem the answer is "none."

I don't buy it. Not only do I believe in a Creator God, but I also believe in a moral God: a great lawgiver, who gave us a perfect moral code. And far from being an outdated set of dos and don'ts from some ancient outmoded religion, the Ten Commandments still remain God's standard for right and wrong today. They're laws that simply make sense.

Just think about the first commandment. It fits right in with this subject, saying very simply, "You shall have no other gods before Me" (Exodus 20:3). Now why would that be the first commandment? It's really simple: it's because there *are* no other gods. He's the one who created us, and so, logically, He's the one we should worship. Right from the start, with that commandment, He set the foundation for everything that follows. He has to come first in our lives because all we have comes from Him.

The famous political activist Bertrand Russell spent time in jail back in 1918 for his opposition to World War I. During a regular prison routine, his jailer, just wanting to strike up idle conversation, asked Bertrand Russell what his religion was. Russell replied that he was an agnostic. So the jailer, not the brightest bulb on the tree, looked a bit puzzled, and then brightened up replying, "I guess it's alright. We all worship the same God, don't we?"

Well, to be honest, no we don't. I know that flys in the face of popular thinking, and maybe it's not fashionable to say it in a global village, but there really is only one God—the God who created the world. And because He's the Creator, He has the right to be first in our lives. That's why, when asked about the greatest commandment, Jesus said:

"You shall love the LORD your God with all your heart, with all your soul, and with all your mind. This is the first and great commandment." (Matthew 22:37, 38)

That's something you just can't do if you have other gods that come ahead of Him.

Notice, too, that Jesus said this was "the first commandment." Doesn't the first commandment read, "You shall have no other gods before Me"? Yes, that's exactly the point. Jesus is basically interpreting the first commandment, saying that it means you will love the Lord your God with everything you have, leaving no room for any other.

I know a man who was married for a number of years. On the surface it all seemed fine; he was a nice family man with a wife and children. Much to our dismay, we discovered that over the years the man had a series of lovers on the side. When the wife found out, she was angry and devastated. So you can imagine how she felt when he tried to explain that, in spite of all those other women, he still loved her with all his heart, his soul, and mind. Of course she rejected that kind of thinking, because when you love someone with everything you have, there's no room for anyone else. That's the way it is with God. It's an exclusive relationship. And it's a relationship that makes very good sense.

In Daniel chapter five the Bible speaks of "… the God who holds your breath in His hand and owns all your ways…" (Daniel 5:23).

Did you notice? "… the God who holds your breath…" That means God didn't just make you—He keeps you alive. He's the God described in the New Testament like this:

"For in Him we live and move and have our being… " (Acts 17:28)

In this God we live, we move, we have our being—our very existence! That's why He has to come first. Why He has to be loved with all our heart, with all our soul, and with all our mind. That's the first great commandment in God's moral law.

You're likely to ask the question, "But what's in it for me?" It might be a selfish question, even an inappropriate one; but still, I know we're going to ask it. The good news is that God's law, from beginning to end, was actually written for your good. Just think about the logic in that first commandment. If there are no other gods, and the Creator God is holding your life together, don't you think it makes good sense to walk in step with Him?

Go into any bookstore, and check out the self-help section. You'll find hundreds, maybe thousands, of books; some of them are pretty good. But not one of them comes anywhere close to the kind of living you'll enjoy when you mold your life to fit God's moral guidelines. After all, they were developed by the One who made you in the first place. The Ten Commandments paint a picture of a remarkably loving God. To live by those principles, you don't need a brain like Einstein's either. Your brain will do just fine.

CHAPTER THREE

The IDOLATORS

In the twenty-first century, when someone thinks of pirates the first thing that often comes to mind is Johnny Depp running around on a pirate ship swinging his sword as a half-competent swashbuckler. The goofy antics of Captain Jack Sparrow can't even begin to depict the horrors that real piracy brought to the unfortunate souls who were victimized by them, however.

Even though piracy became a problem as soon as human beings took to the sea, during the centuries surrounding the time of Christ, piracy was a serious problem in the Mediterranean, making already dangerous sea voyages far more risky than they should have been. Hordes of sea marauders, coming from what is now southeastern Turkey, not only plundered the ships and stole their goods, but also took passengers captive, and sold them into slavery—which proved to be a very lucrative trade. It's been estimated that on one single day pirates sold ten thousand people into slavery, most of them to work on the plantations of rich Roman citizens.

Here's the interesting thing about it. The pirates put the Romans in a real bind. On the one hand, as rulers of the ancient world the Romans were responsible to keep law and order, and to be the guardians of the seas. But on the other hand, they really liked the steady flow of cheap slave labor that they needed for their farms and massive building projects. So over the years they only made occasional half-hearted attempts to deal with pirates. Not until the time of the Emperor Pompey—when strong political considerations forced the Romans to do something—did they finally take any real measures to stop the pirates.

Now the pirates didn't always sell people into slavery. When they got their hands on a wealthy captive, they would hold him for ransom, receiving a lot more money than they would from selling him as a slave. In the middle-to-late first century B.C., the pirates captured a young Roman aristocrat, a man who came to be known as Gaius Julius Caesar. According to the story, when the pirates told their new captive they wanted twenty talents for his release, the young man actually started to laugh. "Twenty talents? Are you kidding me? Don't you know who I am and who my family is? I'm worth more than double that." And at that point, Caesar told them to ask for fifty talents. Naturally, the pirates agreed.

Here's how that played out. Back then you didn't have FedEx or Western Union, so you couldn't wire the money. Because of that it took over a month for the ransom money to come. While they waited, Caesar spent his days schmoozing it up with the pirates, playing their games with them, and cracking a lot of jokes. In fact, history tells us that sometimes he acted as if he were the leader instead of a prisoner.

It's hard to imagine, but Caesar began to call the shots. He wrote songs and poetry on board, and would share them with the pirates. If they didn't like something, he would mock them to their faces, calling them illiterate savages. At night, when he was trying to sleep and the pirates were making noise, he would tell them to quiet down. On more than one occasion, with a gleam in his eye, he told them that he was going to return with ships and hang every single one of them on a Roman cross.

The pirates didn't think much of it, and refused to take him seriously. After all, he was the prisoner, right? That proved to be their biggest mistake. After the ransom was paid, and Julius Caesar was released, he gathered a small fleet of ships, hunted them down, captured most of them, and had every one of them crucified—just as he promised.

It's that type of story that illustrates how Julius Caesar became the kind of man he did. His bravado, skill and determination marked his rise to power, and gave him the resources he needed to preside over one of Rome's greatest military expansions, during which he managed to capture both France and England. With one success after another on almost every front, Julius Caesar became the undisputed ruler of Rome; and really, because Rome ruled the world, he became the undisputed ruler of the world. His statues were adorned like gods, and he even named himself the "unconquerable god." In his mind, he was worthy of the people's worship.

The problem with this situation was that, as his power kept increasing, other people started to get nervous. He was too close to becoming a king, and if the Romans hated one thing, it was the idea of a king ruling them. Eventually they hatched a plot to kill him before he destroyed the Republic and replaced it with a monarchy. To be honest, we don't know exactly what happened, but William Shakespeare supplies us with a discussion between two of the conspirators, Cassius and Brutus. In that discussion Cassius talks about how he once tried to swim across a river with Caesar, and how Caesar got a cramp and he had to save him from drowning. "So how is it," Cassius wondered, "that a mere mortal has to rescue a so-called god?" "And now," said Cassius, "Caesar is considered a god, and Cassius is a wretched creature, and must bow down if Caesar even carelessly nods at him?"

Cassius in recounting another incident, this time in Spain where the great Julius Caesar becomes sick with a fever, says:

When he was having fits, I saw clearly how he shook. It is true, this god shook. His lips turned pale … I heard him groan. Yes, and that tongue of his that persuaded the Romans to watch him closely and write his speeches in their books, cried, "Give me something to drink … " Just like a sick girl!

Cassius asks the question, "What kind of god is this?" The answer is simple: it's a god of human devising—the kind of god who can't save himself, let alone those who put their faith in him. It's the kind of god that people all over the world, in every country and in every century, have managed to create for themselves: a god who can't help them, because he doesn't really exist.

The great Russian writer Dostoyevsky said that human beings must worship something: anything. And whatever we worship—money, fame, power, celebrities, or whatever—these things become our gods, our idols, the things we look up to. We sell our souls for them, and they become the focus of our lives. The problem with idolatry is that we never rise higher than the idols we worship; in fact, we become like the idols we worship. That's a pretty scary thought when you consider who or what some of these idols are.

This book is about the Ten Commandments, and how they still make sense for life in the twenty-first century. Some people have come to the conclusion that not only are the Ten Commandments outdated and outmoded, but that we don't really need *any* kind of moral code for modern life. Instead, people are saying that we can just follow our conscience and do what it tells us. Jean-Jacques Rousseau, the famous French thinker, wrote this:

O Conscience! Conscience! thou divine instinct, thou certain guide of an ignorant and confined, though intelligent and free being;—thou infallible judge of good and evil, who makest man to resemble the Deity.

What was he saying? He is saying that our own minds are powerful enough to form our own moral code, essentially making us our own god.

That kind of thinking is popular today. After all, we're living in what's been called the postmodern era: an era where we all get to march to the beat of a different drummer, where everyone can follow the dictates of whatever resonates with us personally. Each culture, each society, each individual is different, and so, working from different premises, from different backgrounds, we can't really pass judgment on the actions of others. We just do what we think is right.

That type of thinking creates some real sticky problems, however. Maybe you read about the woman in Denver who murdered her own grandchild, because she says she was getting spiritual messages from the geese that were flying above her head. She said the geese told her to do it, and so, following her own conscience, her own sense of right and wrong, she followed their instructions.

I know what you may be thinking. That's a pretty harsh example, and it doesn't really fit what happens in most peoples' lives. You're right—it is a bit extreme. But it makes a point we shouldn't ignore. Let me give you another example. Notice this famous comment:

If there is a God, then He gives us not only life but also consciousness and awareness. If I live my life according to my God-given insights, then I cannot go wrong, and even if I do, I know that I have acted in good faith.

That sounds reasonable, right? If you listen to your heart and follow what your conscience tells you, then you can't go wrong. Frankly, if you have a good internal guide to get you through life, then you shouldn't need a set of rules like the Ten Commandments, correct?

There's just one small problem with the above quotation. That wonderful, rational comment about following the dictates of your conscience came from the mind of Adolph Hitler—and there are very few people who will argue that he was right.

There's just no question that human beings need a moral code that's outside of themselves and their individual cultures. We have one, in the Ten Commandments: a set of laws developed by the Creator God. One of those commandments, the one that is the focus of this chapter, says this:

"You shall not make for yourself a carved image—or any likeness of anything that is in heaven above, or that is in the earth beneath, or that is in the water under the earth; you shall not bow down to them nor serve them. For I, the LORD your God, am a jealous God, visiting the iniquity of the fathers upon the children to the third and fourth generations of those who hate Me, but showing mercy to thousands, to those who love Me and keep My commandments." (Exodus 20:4-6)

You may be wondering just how relevant that commandment is today. How many people still bow down and worship "carved images," especially in our Western Civilization? How many of us know people who bow down and worship images of frogs or goats? And how many of us actually know a pagan sun worshiper?

Actually that's not the point. Anything that becomes the complete focus of our lives, anything that become the supreme object of our love and devotion, anything that rules our souls and comes before the God who created us, becomes an idol: the very thing God warns us about. The reason He gives us a warning is because the worship of idols will eventually destroy us morally and spiritually.

In the history of ancient Israel, the Hebrews were surrounded by idolatrous nations: people who made images of animals, fish, or birds, and then worshipped these idols. I can't help but think that type of worship led directly to the kinds of horrible moral practices associated with that age, things like temple prostitution and child sacrifices.

In other words, if the god you worship is an animal, or a goat, or a fish, or a bird, do you really think you will rise to a higher moral plane than the animal?

I don't know anyone who actually worships the idols of Dagon, the fish god of the Canaanites. But I *do* know a lot of people who worship idols of Andrew Jackson, George Washington, and Abraham Lincoln. I'm not really talking about our famous presidents—I'm talking about the money that bears their portraits.

Americans were shocked by the Enron scandal that led to the

loss of billions of dollars due to the sheer greed of men who already had a lot of money to start with. Even though they were already richer than most of us could imagine, Ken Lay, Andrew Fastow, and Jeffrey Skilling apparently still thought they didn't have enough. To be honest, I don't really know their hearts, but it's hard to deny that for a lot of people money becomes an all-consuming god. We'll throw out our honesty, our morality, our fiscal responsibility, all for the sake of the money god—with innocent people getting hurt in the process. Please don't miss this important point. Read the second commandment again, focusing on the last few lines in particular.

"You shall not make for yourself a carved image—or any likeness of anything that is in heaven above, or that is in the earth beneath, or that is in the water under the earth; you shall not bow down to them nor serve them. For I, the LORD your God, am a jealous God, visiting the iniquity of the fathers upon the children to the third and fourth generations of those who hate Me, but showing mercy to thousands, to those who love Me and keep My commandments." (Exodus 20:4-6)

The last part of this commandment has confused a lot of people. It's not really talking about God punishing someone for something their grandpa did; it's talking about the impact, the result of sins that reach across time and hurt the lives of other people, even three or four generations later. Imagine the suffering that the Enron executives' families have had to live with, and how many years they're going to have to pay the consequences for what happened. But while it's quite easy for us to focus on money, it's not the only idol out there.

We seem to have a special talent for making idols out of anything. Agrippina, the mother of the ancient Roman Emperor Nero, went to an oracle to ask about the future of her boy. The oracle told her he would become the emperor of Rome. But before she could get too excited, the oracle continued. Young Nero would become emperor, but after he did he would kill his own mother. History tells us that Agrippina, so thirsty for power over the empire, said, "Well, let him kill me, as long as he gets to rule."

Do you see what bad spiritual priorities will do? I once read about professional body builders vying for the Mr. Universe title. They were asked by pollsters that if there was a pill which could guarantee them the title, would they take it—even if the pill would kill them three years later? I know it's hard to believe, but half of them said that they would! That really amounts to idolatry: having the wrong priorities and selling your soul for them. No wonder the Bible says what it does:

Do not love the world or the things in the world. If anyone loves the world, the love of the Father is not in him. For all that is in the world—the lust of the flesh, the lust of the eyes, and the pride of life—is not of the Father but is of the world. And the world is passing away, and the lust of it; but he who does the will of God abides forever. (1 John 2:15-17)

Let me ask you, what exactly are idols, other than just things of this world—empty, useless things that don't deserve our worship. I don't pretend to see things like God does, but I imagine that worshiping money, or power, or prestige, or science, or Elvis—those probably seem just as foolish to God as worshiping statues of cats or bulls.

In the book of Isaiah, the Lord had these words for idolaters:

"...I am the First and I am the Last; Besides Me there is no God. ..." Those who make an image, all of them are useless, ... The craftsman stretches out his rule, He marks one out with chalk; He fashions it with a plane, He marks it out with the compass, And makes it like the figure of a man, According to the beauty of a man, that it may remain in the house. He cuts down cedars for himself, And takes the cypress and the oak; He secures it for himself among the trees of the forest. He plants a pine, and the rain nourishes it. Then it shall be for a man to burn, For he will take some of it and warm himself; Yes, he kindles it and bakes bread; Indeed he makes a god and worships it; He makes it a carved image, and falls down to it. He burns half of it in the fire; With this half he eats meat; He roasts a roast,

and is satisfied. He even warms himself and says, "Ah! I am warm, I have seen the fire." And the rest of it he makes into a god, His carved image. He falls down before it and worships it, prays to it and says, "Deliver me, for you are my god!" (Isaiah 44:6, 9, 13-17)

Did you see that? In the end, if you worship something other than God, that's all you're going to have. Is a statue of a bull going to save you from sickness, or death and destruction? Is the statue of a frog going to raise you from the grave on the morning of the resurrection? Is the statue of a goddess going to realize for you the promise of eternal life?

Even though those things are ancient history, it really isn't any different today. What is Michael Jackson going to do for you when your child dies? What is money, fame, or power—all the things that people idolize—going to do for you on your deathbed, when your vital signs are fading fast? What are you going to say? Where are you going to turn? How are you going to pray? "Save me, wealth—after all, I gave my life to you? Save me, power—look at how I worshipped you? Save me, success—I devoted my whole existence to you. Save me, Elvis, save me, Madonna, save me, Tom Cruise!"

Do you see the point? In the end, wealth, power, Madonna, and Tom Cruise are no different than the statues of wood and stone worshipped by the pagans. They're just worldly things, all of which are going to pass away.

That's why the Lord calls us away from worshipping idols, He calls us to worship Him instead, the Life-Giver, the one who created us, who sustains us, and who offers us eternal life through Jesus, His Son. That's something you can stake your future on. The book of Isaiah says:

"I, even I, am the LORD, and besides Me there is no savior." (Isaiah 43:11)

That's the whole point. There is no Savior besides the Lord Jesus Christ, and He alone can bring you the promise of life at the end of the age. He's the only One who can bring your loved ones back from the grave. And He's the only One who sacrificed Himself on the cross for you. That's why only God should be worshipped.

It's not too late to shift your focus, and create new priorities that can literally save your life. Walk away from the idols, and let God spare you from the heartache and devastation that they will eventually bring. Give your heart back to God. I guarantee, you're going to find out what it really means to live.

CHAPTER FOUR

Thou Shalt Not Be a RELIGOUS HYPOCRITE

He was one of the biggest televangelists in the history of religious broadcasting. By the mid-1980s, his weekly show was watched by millions of people all around the world. In fact, it's been estimated that about eight million people watched him every single week. To be perfectly honest, this man was wealthy too, because his ministry took in about 150 million dollars a year as folks responded to his impassioned sermons, especially the ones against sexual immorality.

In fact, when the whole PTL scandal broke a couple of decades ago, this preacher had some pretty tough words for fellow TV evangelist Jim Bakker, who was caught trying to pay $265,000 in hush money to a woman he'd been having an affair with. He called Bakker, "A cancer in the body of Christ."

One year before that, he was also involved in uncovering the immorality of a fellow minister in his own denomination. His track record proved that he was absolutely uncompromising, unwavering, in his battle against sin.

With one tiny little exception. He was tough on other people's sins, but on his own…well, it turns out he wasn't quite so tough. In fact, all the while he was preaching so vehemently against sexual immorality, it turns out that he was personally visiting prostitutes, looking at dirty pictures, and at the same time leading the charge for stricter laws against pornography.

If you check the dictionary there's actually a word for this kind of behavior—when you preach one thing and live another. It's "hypocrisy." To be honest, a lot of the world is sick and tired of seeing it within the Christian church.

It seems like every year we have a new scandal, where somebody who preaches against sexual immorality or the evils of money turns out to be partaking in it himself. I don't really want to stand in judgment on these people, because in the final analysis that privilege belongs to God. But at the same time, as case after case is spread across the evening news, we need to call it what it is: one of the greatest of all human sins.

I realize that the word "hypocrite" gets thrown around a lot. It can be used to describe all sorts of behavior. I suppose that to some degree or other, or at some time or another, everybody has been guilty. But the worst form of hypocrisy, the one that really appalls, is religious hypocrisy: the person who tries to disguise his or her own personal defects under the guise of holiness and self-righteousness. Frankly, the problem is so serious that the Bible deals with it in very specific terms. There's even a whole commandment in the moral code of God that deals with it.

Exactly which commandment says, "You shall not be a religious hypocrite?" Well, to be perfectly honest, none of them. At least not in those words; but you can find the principle buried in the third commandment, which reads:

"You shall not take the name of the LORD your God in vain, for the LORD will not hold him guiltless who takes His name in vain." *(Exodus 20:7)*

At first glance, most people believe this is a commandment against using God's name as a curse word, and that is certainly a part of it. But it's only a small part. If you study it carefully, you'll find there's something much, much deeper going on. The deeper meaning is found in the small word, "vain." You shall not take the name of the Lord your God in vain.

What exactly does that mean? The Hebrew word for vain in this commandment basically means "nothingness," or "vanity," or "emptiness," or "worthless." What it's saying is that you shouldn't utilize God's name in a worthless way. Don't use God's name—don't profess God's name—as if it means nothing. Don't claim to be a follower of God unless you live like a follower of God. Don't go around using the name of God, and all that it entails, unless you are going to live like you mean it. Don't cover your personal sins in the name of a God who never, ever, sanctions your sins. Don't defile the name of the Lord. In short, don't be a religious hypocrite.

It's one thing when you hear stories about people who do bad things and get caught. But when someone who has great privileges and great responsibilities is caught doing the very same things, it just seems all that much worse. When some poor adolescent, living on the "wrong side of the tracks" without much hope for a better life, sticks up a liquor store, that's bad enough. But when the son of the most prominent man in town holds up the same liquor store, for some reason it just seems worse. What the Bible is saying with this commandment is essentially, "If you are going to profess to be of a follower of God, if you are going to cover yourself with the exalted mantle of His name, if you are going to be known as one of God's children, then be prepared to live like it."

There's the story of a bank robber in Israel who, even though he was right handed, always held his gun in his left hand during a robbery. He did this so, as he ran out of the bank with the loot, he could still perform the pious act of touching the mezuzah (a small object kept on doorposts to remind Jews of God's law) as he fled from the scene of the crime. Now that's a great example of taking the name of the Lord in vain!

Christian speaker Tony Campolo tells the story of being mugged at gunpoint. After the robber took his wallet he asked his victim, "What kind of work do you do?" Tony answered, "I'm a Baptist minister." "Oh," said the thief, "you're a Baptist? So am I." Another brilliant example of taking the name of the Lord in vain.

In the city of Rome a man held a priest at gunpoint. Trying to calm the robber, the priest asked him if he wanted a cigar. "Oh, no, Father," he said, "I can't do that. I've given up smoking for Lent." The hypocrisy is obvious. He wasn't living what his religion professed, and that means that he was taking the name of God in vain.

I know a Christian who wanted to witness to his mother, a non-Christian, about Jesus. He tried to be the best example he could, always putting Jesus in the best possible light. Just when he thought he was making some progress, his mother started going out with a Mafioso. This guy would kill people; yet every Sunday he not only went to church, but he insisted that my friend's mother go with him! You've got to wonder—what's the point? It's just taking the Lord's name in vain!

Let's be honest, in the past few decades in America, there's been a pretty disturbing trend. Christians are starting to notice that the level of morality in this country is really sliding. It bothers them to the point where they want to take the reigns of government and do something about it. When it comes to the moral problems in society, I'd have to agree; we're seriously slipping. But what's very disturbing is what the polls show about Christians themselves. In the areas of basic immorality—lying, cheating, stealing, and so on—professed Christians, the ones who take God's name, are doing exactly the same things. In fact, in some polls we've discovered that practical morality among Christians is no better than the people who live around them. I read one study, basically making fun of Christians, which showed that when Christians meet for big conventions, more X-rated movies are rented in hotel rooms than when other groups meet.

What's my point? Well, instead of worrying about everyone else, maybe Christians need to start at home. Maybe it's time we took a serious look at the third commandment. Just think about how different things would be if everybody who claimed to be a Christian and took on the name of God really meant it. What would happen if Christians actually lived by the principles that Jesus taught? Just think about how much better our homes and marriages would be. Think about how much better our relationship would be with our children, our co-workers, and our friends if we only took the name of God on ourselves and lived it.

It's likely you were as shocked as I was at the tragic killing of five Amish schoolgirls in the fall of 2006. The thought of those little girls in their long dresses and bonnets being murdered in cold blood really tears your heart out. You've got to wonder, how could anybody do that?

But you know what really astounded me, what taught me an incredible lesson in living the Christian faith? At the same time the Amish people were grieving over their children, they were calling for their own people to forgive the man who did it! Imagine: the grandfather of one of those dead girls stood in front of her casket and said, "We are teaching our young people not to think evil of this man." In fact, some of the Amish people even attended the funeral of the killer. And more than that, some of them offered help and support to his wife and family.

What a powerful testimony to what it means to be a follower of Jesus. I don't know for sure, but I imagine that the story of those Amish people forgiving the killer and reaching out to his family probably did more to advance the cause of Christianity than a thousand sermons preached on any topic. Try to imagine what our world would be like if everyone were that forgiving!

On the other hand, look at the damage religious hypocrisy has done to the cause of Christ. I heard about a Christian who years ago befriended an old Jewish man. He grew very friendly with his new friend, and when he thought the time was right he started to share something about Jesus. Immediately, as soon as he mentioned the name of Christ, the old man became cold, and almost hostile.

The Christian was a little confused. "Have I offended you?"

"Yes," said the old man, "because when I lived in the old country, a group of church-going people came into our village, and with the blessings of the priest who wore a big cross on his neck, started killing the men and sexually assaulting the women. I watched my father hung from a tree, and my own mother was violated. They all claimed to be followers of Jesus; so please, spare me your Jesus."

There's a story about Alexander the Great. He was told about a soldier who had been a coward in battle. Alexander the Great came to him and asked him his name. The man, with a sudden flash of hope, said, "My name is Alexander, just like yours!" At which point, Alexander the Great looked at him and said, "If you are going to act like that, either change your name or live like someone who carries my name." Can you see why the third commandment is so important?

Jesus dealt with hypocrites differently from other sinners, and there's a good reason. As you read the Bible, you find that He worked with a lot of people we might be tempted to call "low-lifes"; people like prostitutes and other outcasts. Yet, without condoning what these people did, He had better words for them than the religious hypocrites, those who hid their sins under robes of self-righteousness.

In talking to the religious establishment of His day Jesus said:

"But woe to you, scribes and Pharisees, hypocrites! For you shut up the kingdom of heaven against men; for you neither go in yourselves, nor do you allow those who are entering to go in. Woe to you, scribes and Pharisees, hypocrites! For you devour widows' houses, and for a pretense make long

prayers. Therefore you will receive greater condemnation. Woe to you, scribes and Pharisees, hypocrites! For you travel land and sea to win one proselyte, and when he is won, you make him twice as much a son of hell as yourselves. ...Woe to you, scribes and Pharisees, hypocrites! For you pay tithe of mint and anise and cummin, and have neglected the weightier matters of the law: justice and mercy and faith. These you ought to have done, without leaving the others undone. Blind guides, who strain out a gnat and swallow a camel! Woe to you, scribes and Pharisees, hypocrites! For you cleanse the outside of the cup and dish, but inside they are full of extortion and self-indulgence. Blind Pharisee, first cleanse the inside of the cup and dish, that the outside of them may be clean also. Woe to you, scribes and Pharisees, hypocrites! For you are like whitewashed tombs which indeed appear beautiful outwardly, but inside are full of dead men's bones and all uncleanness. Even so you also outwardly appear righteous to men, but inside you are full of hypocrisy and lawlessness." (Matthew 23:13-15, 23-28)

Wow! That's pretty direct, don't you think? Even the evangelist who condemned Jim Bakker didn't speak like that. You don't find the gospels recording Jesus talking that way to prostitutes or thieves, either. This kind of language was reserved for those who took His name in vain. He condemned them for devouring the houses of widows, taking their property, yet at the same time cloaking their deeds under a veneer of long prayers, as if their long prayers somehow negated the sinfulness of their actions. He rebuked them for performing all kinds of small religious rituals that supposedly made them look holy and pious, even though they neglected kindness, mercy, and compassion. He chided them for their obsession with outward ritualistic cleanliness that accompanied the Jewish dietary laws, while on the inside their minds and hearts were full of greed and self-indulgence.

At the core, all these men were violating the third commandment. "You shall not take the name of the LORD your God in vain." You shall not do wrong things while trying to cover it up in the name of God.

Taking God's name in vain refers to people who put on the veneer of godliness in public, and live like the devil behind closed doors. It applies to people who claim to know God, but live like they're more familiar with the world. Jesus talks about it in no uncertain terms in Matthew chapter seven:

"Not everyone who says to Me, 'Lord, Lord,' shall enter the kingdom of heaven, but he who does the will of My Father in heaven. Many will say to Me in that day, 'Lord, Lord, have we not prophesied in Your name, cast out demons in Your name, and done many wonders in Your name?' And then I will declare to them, 'I never knew you; depart from Me, you who practice lawlessness!'" (Matthew 7:21-23)

He was speaking to people who called on the Lord, and even supposedly did wonderful things in His name, but still Jesus calls them workers of iniquity. The Greek word for "iniquity" is literally defined as "lawlessness," which means that these people, even though they used God's name, were not obeying His law. And that's hypocrisy, plain and simple.

And that's only the first part of the commandment. After telling us not to take His name in vain, the Lord ends the commandment with: "... for the LORD will not hold him guiltless who takes His name in vain" (Exodus 20:7).

That means that, in the end, you're not going to get away with it. The Lord will not hold him guiltless who uses His holy name as a cover for lawlessness; He will not hold him guiltless who uses His holy name to condemn others and yet is guilty of the same sin they condemn; He will not hold him guiltless who takes God's holy name, but in that name commits actions that the Lord would never give His blessing to. That's a very serious matter don't you think?

Let me make one thing perfectly clear before I go any further. I'm a minister, and for that matter, an evangelist. I publicly profess to be a follower of Jesus Christ. Every day I do things in the name of the Lord. But right up front, I have to admit that I am also a sinner. I guarantee that if you hold my life under the magnifying glass, you're likely to find something. The same thing is true of you—but that doesn't automatically make you a hypocrite.

You see, the third commandment doesn't condemn you for not being all that you should be. It simply calls us to be the best we can through Jesus. But still, my best just isn't good enough, and it never will be; which is why I still need Jesus as my Savior. I hope you can see the difference. Just because you aren't perfect, you aren't a hypocrite. Hypocrisy is different. It's pretending to be more than you really are.

The real issue you need to face for today is that, although you aren't perfect, God's perfect Son gave His life for you. Because of that you can turn around. Jesus offers you His perfect life instead of your imperfect one.

Let your sins drive you to the cross, not away from it. For you, for anyone open to Him, there's forgiveness, healing, and the chance for a new life through Jesus—even for those who have violated this all-important third commandment. Standing in Jesus, admitting your mistakes, is not hypocrisy. The Bible calls it eternal life.

CHAPTER FIVE

A "Place" IN TIME

It was a cold December day, and even though the air was crisp, a crowd was gathering. Anticipation grew as each moment passed. For young Pierre standing in the crowd, the excitement was overwhelming. If everything went according to plan, he was going to witness history in the making. In just a few moments, the world record for land speed would be broken, right in front of his eyes.

Speculation abounded, especially in the press. Could a human being really move that fast on land and survive? Could the vehicle really travel at these amazing speeds without falling apart? Everyone weighed in on the discussions, from automobile engineers to doctors.

In just moments the questions would all be answered—forever. And Pierre was going to witness it!

A collective gasp rose from the crowd when the car was finally brought out. Pierre had never seen anything like it. What an incredible machine! It looked like something out of science fiction—from out of the future. With a sense of utter admiration, and not a small amount of apprehension, he watched the driver, all suited up, climb into the vehicle.

When the engine started, Pierre was sure he felt the ground shake. The engine roared. It was unbelievable. Soon all was set and ... zoom! The car took off, building up speed by the second. Pierre, along with everyone else watching, just couldn't believe how fast it went.

When it was over, both the car and driver were fine, much to everyone's relief and satisfaction. When the news of the final speed was announced, a gasp of astonishment rose from the crowd, followed by loud cheering. A new world record had been set. The year was 1898, and the car had gone just a little over 39 miles per hour.

That's right, 39.24 mph. Today, when some elderly lady, whose forehead barely makes it up to the dashboard, is creeping along the highway at 50 mph, we become easily frustrated and many are tempted to swear. But back in 1898 the world was astonished when someone traveled 39.24 mph.

You've got to wonder just what all those people would think of the latest land speed record, set in 1997, when a jet-powered car roared across the Nevada desert at more than 763 mph. Of course, it's only a matter of time until someone manages to go even faster than that. There's just something about humans that won't let us rest until we can move just a little bit faster. No matter how fast we get, and how efficient we become, it's just never enough.

Maybe you remember those old-time phones where you actually had to dial the number. You had to go through the annoyance of putting your finger in a little hole and turning a dial clockwise seven times to make a phone call. The whole process would take ten or fifteen seconds every time. Thinking that it took way too long, someone developed push button telephones, enabling dialing at a fraction of the time. Now we also have speed dial—so we only have to push one button. I'm not a licensed futurist, but I'm guessing that before too long, somebody's going to come up with something better than that. It just seems to be wired into our system.

Take a look at the whole phenomenon of home computers. My first computer ran at about 133 megahertz, but my new one runs about thirty times faster. And even though I can't imagine why I could possibly need it, the computer industry is already coming out with machines that run even faster. Which leads some people to feel that the minute they take their new computer out of the box, it's already outdated.

There's just no question about it; we're doing things faster and faster, at speeds our ancestors couldn't even have imagined. If you wanted to get a message across the Atlantic two hundred years ago, it would take weeks at best. But today you can push ten or twelve buttons, and in seconds be talking to someone across the Atlantic. I doubt that a few hundred years ago people could even dream of a world like this, yet we take it for granted.

A while back I was flying from Toronto to Los Angeles, a trip that would normally take about four and a half hours. There was a delay before take off, and the pilot came over the intercom saying, "It will be just a few more minutes, folks, then we'll be taking off. Thank you for your patience." You know what that means. It took a couple more hours to get the plane off the ground. In the end it took seven hours to fly from Toronto to Los Angeles. I was actually irritated at the delay. Yet two hundred years ago, that same trip would have taken me a month.

You see it? We're moving way too fast, and no matter how fast we get, we still want more. Here's the really strange part: even though we're operating at speeds our ancestors would have deemed miraculous, even supernatural, most people still complain about the same thing—they just don't have enough time. We're all burned out because no matter what we do or how fast we do it, and no matter where we go or how fast we get there, there's still more to do and more places to go, and just not enough time. If days had thirty hours instead of twenty-four, I still doubt we'd feel like we had enough time. The bottom line is, time is something of a tyrant, a dictator that demands everything we have. The sad fact is we never seem to have enough to satisfy our brutal taskmaster.

That's a problem God actually anticipated. Thousands of years ago, God gave us a commandment specifically created to protect us from the tyranny of time. At the very beginning of our human history, the Lord carved out an inviolable and indestructible refuge called the Sabbath. As you trace the fourth commandment through the annals of time, you'll find it comes to us right from the opening chapters of the Bible, in the story of Creation.

In the first pages of the first book, Genesis, we read:

Thus the heavens and the earth, and all the host of them, were finished. And on the seventh day God ended His work which He had done, and He rested on the seventh day from all His work which He had done. Then God blessed the seventh day and sanctified it, because in it He rested from all His work which God had created and made. (Genesis 2:1-3)

Now follow me carefully. I've heard some people say that the fourth commandment no longer applies to us, and usually for one of two reasons. First, some people say that the Sabbath was part of the ceremonial rituals of the Jews, and that it should be grouped with things like the animal sacrifices that pointed to Christ as the sacrifice for our sin. The argument goes that since Christ has come, and all those sacrificial rituals have been abolished, then the Sabbath commandment is finished, too. And up to a point, they're right. The sacrificial rituals are done away with, because we no longer need them. But to say the Sabbath was part of it is simply wrong. What was abolished was all ceremonial; part of the sacrificial system established by God to teach us how He deals with sin. But the Bible shows us that God rested and blessed the seventh day before sin ever came into the picture, so it can't possibly be part of the ritual system.

Second, some have said that the Sabbath commandment was only for the Jews, and sometimes it is called the "Jewish Sabbath." But that raises a very important question. How can the seventh day be the "Jewish Sabbath" when it came from the Garden of Eden and existed for thousands of years before the Jews? God blessed the seventh day long before a single Jew existed, so you know it can't be an exclusive Jewish institution. This is one of the reasons that Jesus said that the Sabbath was made for "man." It wasn't made for only the Jews; it was made for all of us.

You will find it at the heart of the Ten Commandments, the moral code for the human race:

"Remember the Sabbath day, to keep it holy. Six days you shall labor and do all your work, but the seventh day is the Sabbath of the LORD your God. In it you shall do no work: you, nor your son, nor your daughter, nor your male servant, nor your female servant, nor your cattle, nor your stranger who is *within your gates. For* in *six days the LORD made the heavens and the earth, the sea, and all that* is *in them, and rested the seventh day. Therefore the LORD blessed the Sabbath day and hallowed it."*
(Exodus 20:8-11)

I want you to notice how this commandment is directly linked to the original six-day creation story from the book of Genesis. God tells us to rest because He sanctified and made the Sabbath day holy, almost the exact wording used in Genesis. That's why God says to "remember" the Sabbath, because it's something that already existed. But it's also the only commandment that starts with the word "remember," probably because it's about the easiest one for us to forget. When my wife tells me to "remember" to take out the trash, or to "remember" to bring something home from work, it's because she knows I'm liable to forget. I suspect it might be the same way with this fourth commandment.

But what I really want you to think about is this: there's a reason for this commandment. If you study the other nine, you quickly discover that all of them are for our good. The same is true with number four. If we would only listen to God a little more carefully, our lives would simply be better. No matter how fast we move, how much faster our computers become, how much faster our cell phones will connect us to the world, or how much faster we can eat our meals—we just never seem to have enough time to "feed the beast." But then you open the Bible to the Ten Commandments, and you find God asking us to take time to rest.

We should notice that God isn't really making a suggestion here: He's *commanding* us to rest, to devote one seventh of our lives to it. It's just as much a commandment of God as the prohibitions against murder, adultery, and stealing. That's because God knows that if we were left on our own, we would never take a break from the ceaseless flow of time. We would simply work, and work, and work, and do, and do, and do, until we worked ourselves to death. God knows there will never be enough time. So, once a week, God gives us a break—a refuge from the tyranny of time.

Just think about this. Life is so full of stress and strain. We always have to hustle just to stay afloat. And so often—in the rush to make money, to advance our careers, to get ahead—who gets left behind but the very people we wanted to enjoy the fruits of our success in the first place, our loved ones: our family, our spouse and our children.

With the Sabbath, God is giving us a special place in time, a sacred place where the things of the world—the boss, the bills, the chores—are not allowed to intrude, because this is sacred and holy time. Imagine someone named Max. Max is a self-made millionaire, a man who went from rags to riches through sheer grit and determination. If you define success the way most people do, you'd have to say that Max was a really big success, especially when you look at his bank account. But it's toward the end of his life, and Max is looking back and thinking that he has one big regret. "If only," he says, "if only I had spent less time with my family: my wife, my children, and my grandkids, and more time in the office."

You can tell I made Max up, because that just doesn't happen. Who in their right mind, when he gets to the end of his life, would ever wish he had spent less time with his family? I can tell you for sure that it's usually the other way around. And that's why the Sabbath is such good news: it gives us a block of time, every single week without exception, that can be dedicated in a special way to the people we love.

There's something else fascinating about the Sabbath commandment. Remember how I mentioned that it really came before sin, at the foundation of the world? Interestingly enough, there's one other institution that comes from the Garden of Eden, just like the Sabbath: the institution of marriage. Adam and Eve were husband and wife before the problem of sin. That means that the Sabbath and marriage both date back to the birth of the world. If you study it, you'll find that both of them are about relationships. By not allowing the things of this world to intrude on that time, the Sabbath gives us a valuable resource to help develop our marriage relationships.

The same thing is true for your children. Especially when children are young, the Sabbath provides a special time for them to spend with their parents. This is important because adult responsibilities take away from the time that children need and want with their parents. Ask yourself: How many children grow up resentful that their parents were busy with everything in the world except with them? The Sabbath provides an antidote because, if observed correctly, it doesn't allow "everything in the world" to intrude. The bottom line is that the Sabbath provides us with the opportunity to build the one thing that so many of us need, and that's good relationships.

It also means time for the most important relationship of all, the one you have with God. A lot of Christians tell me they just don't have time for a good spiritual life. Yet here it is, right in the fourth commandment. God has set aside a whole day every week for you to get to know Him better.

When you come to the end of your life, you're never going to regret the time you devoted to your relationships with God, your spouse, or your children. Nobody crosses the finish line feeling sorry that they built the relationships that make life worth living. And nobody comes to the end feeling sorry they spent so much time with their God.

Every time this commandment comes up, someone seems to think of it as "legalistic." But I've got to say it sounds pretty good to me. A whole day off from worry, stress, and fear, every single week! I know that some people will try to say that the only reason anybody would ever keep the Sabbath is because they're trying to get brownie points with God and earn their way to heaven—but that just means they haven't really read the Bible. It's absolutely impossible to earn your way into heaven. The only remedy for sin is Jesus Christ and His perfect obedience to the law, which is credited to us by faith. As Paul wrote in Romans 3:20-22:

Therefore by the deeds of the law no flesh will be justified in His sight, for by the law is the knowledge of sin. But now the righteousness of God apart from the law is revealed, being witnessed by the Law and the Prophets, even the righteousness of God, through faith in Jesus Christ, to all and on all who believe....

There's no question; we obey God's law not to be saved, but because we *are* saved. We obey the law because God asks us to, and because it will give us a better life if we obey it, pure and simple. The fourth commandment is all about rest: in the Sabbath we rest from our works, we rest from things of the world, we rest in Jesus and what He has done for us.

Let me ask you a really important question: do you need rest? Not just from the daily grind, not just from the tyranny of time, but rest from guilt, from sin, from the knowledge that you have not been what you really should be? Do you need rest from the burdens that are weighing on your heart and soul? I know of only one answer, and that's Jesus, who says to each of us,

"Come to Me, all you who labor and are heavy laden, and I will give you rest." (Matthew 11:28)

CHAPTER SIX

The Most "Natural" COMMANDMENT

Nate Ybanz grew up in a living nightmare. It wasn't just the vicious and violent beatings his father gave him, as bad as they were. And believe me, the beatings were bad. When Nate was eight years old, his father pummeled him for not mopping the floor the way he wanted him to, and on another occasion, he yanked his son off a lawn mower and beat him for not mowing the grass straight.

But in addition to the beatings, there was other abuse. Over and over his parents told him how useless he was. Then, as if to underscore the point, both his parents abused him sexually. When Nate would reach out for help from doctors, the police, or other kids' families, most of the time his pleas went completely unheeded; which only proved to Nate that he really wasn't worth anything. It wasn't any one of these things alone that drove Nate to desperate measures. It was all of them put together, year after year, which eventually drove sixteen-year-old Nate to take his mother's life.

Family life has changed so much in the last fifty or sixty years that we often refer to the 1950s family sitcom *Leave It To Beaver* as a joke. That's because even though most of us will never have to face the problems faced by Nate Ybanz, the way we grow up now is so radically different from the way Americans grew up then, that we have trouble thinking of a family we know that lives as peaceably and compatibly as the Cleavers from the TV show, *Leave it to Beaver.*

Dysfunctional families didn't begin in the late twentieth Century, however. One of the most famous cases of family dysfunction dates all the way back to the Emperor Nero, who wanted his own mother dead because of the way she continually interfered in the politics of the empire. According to history, he thought about poisoning her, or just putting her to the sword, or doing anything that would get rid of her without implicating him. Finally Nero got an idea. He invited her to a big banquet on the other side of a lake, even arranging for a boat to take her there. If everything went according to plan, the boat would be sabotaged, and she would drown in a "terrible accident." Well, the boat sank exactly as planned, but his mother was rescued. Fed up, and just wanting her gone, Nero sent soldiers to her house, and while she was resting on a couch they beat her to death. Again, not exactly *Leave it to Beaver*, is it?

So what's my point? These stories force us to think very carefully about the fifth commandment: the one about honoring your parents. Where exactly do we draw the line? Most of us will never face the extreme examples illustrated here. It doesn't matter who you are though, everybody has challenging issues when it comes to family life. Nobody has an absolutely perfect relationship with his or her parents, no matter how good it is. Which is why, frankly, God needs to remind us to honor our parents. It's a commandment we violate on a regular basis, even if not to the extreme of Emperor Nero, or a twenty-first century teenager who takes the life of his mother.

But before we look at the commandment itself, I have a question. Why is it that we find the murder of one's parents such a horrible story? Why, exactly, do we feel revulsion or disgust when we hear that somebody killed his mom or dad? Or why are we horrified when we discover that a mother betrays the trust of her children by strapping them into a car and pushing them into a lake, as in the famous case of Susan Smith?

Unless we admit that there are universal moral principles in our world, rules that apply to everybody, we have a massive problem in trying to condemn the breakdown of family relationships. Postmodern thinkers are telling us that we have no real objective moral standards any more, but the horrific headlines in the evening news tell us that's not true. Even postmodern thinkers have to admit that beating your kids, or sexually abusing them is wrong. What they have trouble defining is *why* it's wrong.

The usual reason given is because those kinds of actions hurt people. We then face another problem in logic, because we now have to define why hurting people is wrong. Usually the only defense the postmoderns can give is, "It's wrong because it just is, and everybody agrees on that."

But that kind of thinking breaks down quickly. If we say that hurting people is wrong because most people agree that it's wrong, does that mean that the majority rules when it comes to right and wrong? Does it mean that if everybody agrees on something, that makes it right? Don't forget that before the Civil War we had an awful lot of people who seemed to agree that human slavery was right. Today we all know better than that, at least for the most part, in the Western world.

Again the question comes up: *Why* do we all know better than that? Why is it that we just seem to know—intuitively—that some things are right and other things are wrong? If you think about it, it doesn't really make sense for living beings that are basically carbon, water, and hydrogen to have a sense of right and wrong. Maybe that's why Jean-Paul Sartre, the twentieth century's most influential atheist, said, "It is very distressing that God does not exist, because all possibility of finding values in a heaven of ideas disappears along with Him; there can no longer be a priori Good, since there is no infinite and perfect consciousness to think it." In basic English, he was admitting that without a Creator God, there's really no such thing as right and wrong.

The philosopher Bertrand Russell wrote that "many traditional ethical concepts are difficult to interpret, and many traditional ethical concepts are difficult to justify, except on the assumption that there is a God or a World Spirit, or at least an immanent cosmic Purpose." Again, he's admitting that if you take God out of the equation, you don't really have a sense of right and wrong.

Atheist apologist John L. Mackie argued that, "Moral properties constitute so odd a cluster of qualities and relations that are most unlikely to have arisen in the ordinary course of events without an all-powerful God to create them." And while he wasn't ready to admit the existence of God, he at least admitted the problem we face when we take Him out of the picture. Without God you have a terrible problem trying to define what's right.

And I confess, I must agree with these prominent atheists. The whole idea of morality can't exist without God, because Darwinian biochemistry alone just can't provide us with a sense of good and evil. But quite apart from the famous atheists, I not only believe that God gave us a sense of morality, He also spelled it out in a written code, a code that's found eloquently stated in the Ten Commandments. This chapter is on the fifth commandment, found in Exodus chapter 20:

"Honor your father and your mother, that your days may be long upon the land which the LORD your God is giving you." (Exodus 20:12)

At first glance this is a strange commandment, because you'd think that most people, in most situations, just naturally love their Mom and Dad. I've got two little girls who love their Daddy, and I don't have to tell them to do it—it just kind of happens all by itself. So to find a commandment telling us to merely honor our parents when most of us *love* them seems a little strange, doesn't it? I mean, to tell someone who loves his parents to honor them almost seems like telling someone who's dying of thirst to lick the condensation off a glass of water when what they naturally want to do is drink the whole thing. The commandment almost seems to be setting the bar just a little too low, in some people's opinion. So why does God have to give us a command to do what for most people comes naturally?

Maybe it has something to do with the way our world has gone. Because of the prideful corruption in the human heart, most of our interpersonal relationships have been twisted and damaged beyond recognition. We now have family situations that previous generations had trouble imagining.

Here is a striking example. In 1988 Bill Wyman, of the Rolling Stones, who was 52 at the time, married Mandy Smith, who was only 19. That in itself isn't so unusual, because we have lots of people marrying that are years apart in age. The really strange part was that when they got married, Bill's son Stephan was engaged to Mandy's mother. Follow me carefully: Bill's marriage to Mandy ended before his son married the mother, but if they had stayed together, Bill would have been Stephan's dad and stepson all at the same time, and Mandy's mother would have also been her daughter-in-law.

The point? Modern life is getting pretty complicated, and even though you probably don't face that kind of situation yourself, chances are, if you're living in America, you're probably not living the life of *Leave it to Beaver* either. Because our world has been so severely twisted by sin, and because we're having a hard time defining what's normal, we really do need commandments that teach us how to relate to our families. In the new styles of living, not everything is as obvious as it used to be. We've started to move the markers of normalcy. Without clear guidelines from Someone outside of ourselves, how are we supposed to figure out what's right?

Notice something else. The fifth commandment does not tell us to "like" our mother and father, even though you'd think it would. Reading it carefully you'll notice it only says to "honor" them. So why would God omit something like this?

I suppose it's because God, knowing how messed up we are because of sin, knew that some people wouldn't, or couldn't, or maybe even shouldn't, bring themselves to like everybody.

Let's take a moment to face the hard realities of life in the twenty-first century. I know that many of you don't have to live with the awful things your neighbor has to endure, but it's real life. You can't expect a twelve-year-old girl, whose own family members gave her AIDS, to like them. A boy whose father beat him into a coma with a baseball bat can't be told to like his dad. Honoring him would be hard enough.

God fully anticipated the realities of modern life. Even though most of us aim higher than simply honoring our parents, God provides a realistic baseline for us. Honoring your parents is something you do even when you have trouble mustering positive feelings about how they treated you.

Fortunately a lot of you can easily love your parents. It's not hard, because you had a great time growing up, with godly parents who poured themselves out in an effort to raise you right. But for those of you who didn't have great parents, for those of you who suffered a lot, this commandment draws a new line in the sand for you to live by, now. You don't have to let bitterness rob you of the rest of your life. By the grace of God you can honor your parents without condoning what they did, or putting yourself back in danger. Furthermore, you can do something about your family situation now, by recognizing the high standards that God has for you as a parent.

This commandment tells us that the family is the basic unit, the foundation, of all human society. God expects us to preserve that unit to the best of our ability. Even after children are grown and gone, family bonds are still important. By honoring your parents, you acknowledge those bonds. Then later in life, when the roles have been switched and the children need to take care of their parents, those bonds become even more important.

Who hasn't read, time and time again, about famous and rich people, who have everything the world could offer, and yet are miserable? It's almost a cliché. What's the cause of their misery? It's not that they don't have money. It's not that they don't have fame. It's not that they don't have health or power. Rather it's that they are missing good family relationships.

Artie Shaw, the famous bandleader from the 1940s and 1950s, was married to some of Hollywood's most glamorous women—but all those marriages ended in grief. In an interview towards the end of his life, he was talking about his lousy relationships, and the strained interactions he had with the children from all these different women. He said something to the effect of, "Well, I didn't get along with their mothers, so why should I have gotten along with the kids?"

That's just not God's ideal for us. I hope you see the point: we've passed through a couple of generations now with broken-down family relationships, and the whole of our society is paying the price. Kids don't grow up with the security they were intended to have. Parents aren't reaping the joy that kids are supposed to bring. And all the while, God intended us to have something more. The life of *Leave it to Beaver* might seem kind of corny, but it's no small coincidence that a lot of people are starting to wish their lives were more like it. Do we make fun of that show because we really don't want that kind of life, or are we nervously laughing, because while we know we don't have it, we secretly wish we did?

Right at the heart of God's commandments, we discover that the Creator is family-oriented. It's not just a coincidence that we live in families, and that God Himself describes His essence as three Persons in one God. He's a God of relationships, and when you structure your relationships by the Creator's rules, you will find the joy He intends for you to have.

Family ties really do matter. Centuries after Moses received the commandments from God on the mountain, the Apostle Paul picks up on the fifth commandment and expounds and expands on it:

Children, obey your parents in the Lord, for this is right. "Honor your father and mother," which is the first commandment with promise: "that it may be well with you and you may live long on the earth." And you, fathers, do not provoke your children to wrath, but bring them up in the training and admonition of the Lord. (Ephesians 6:1-4)

Here it is, God's ideal. Just try to imagine what would happen if we lived by it, even on the days when we don't feel like it. I want you to notice something interesting. Paul's initial emphasis is on the children: obey your parents, and honor them. But then he turns to parents, particularly the father, and tells them not to provoke their children. The commandment is a two-way street.

We not only have a responsibility to honor our own parents, but we have a God-given duty to be the kind of parents that our kids will love to honor. Try to imagine how much better our homes, our families, our lives would be were all parents to love and nurture and treat their children well, and in response the children did the same thing to their parents—all their lives!

This means there's hope. If you've had nothing but disastrous relationships, if your own parents were hard to love, and right now you seem to have a terrible family life because of it, you can do something about it. You can give your children the gift of having a Mom or a Dad who is easy to love, and a privilege to honor. You can stop the cycle right now, and give your children, and your grandchildren, a fighting chance at finding the joy that God intended them to have in family relationships.

And the wonderful part of it is this: as you pour yourself into your children, and you love them the way that God loves you, you're going to find that you reap every bit as much benefit as they do. It's a perfectly designed model where God intended to give you the best life possible. If you just put your family in God's hands, and trust that He knows what He's talking about, you're going to find the joy He wanted you to have.

The message of the fifth commandment is simple. God cares about our families, and He wants us to have strong relationships that bring joy and meaning to our lives. For some of you, the damage has already been done. You haven't been great parents, or you didn't have great parents, or you haven't been good to your parents. Sometimes the damage is hard to repair.

But it's never too late to heal your relationship with your heavenly Father. It's never too late for you to turn your heart to the One who loves you with a love greater than any parent has ever had for any child. Whoever you are, whatever your background, your mistakes, your sins, Jesus Christ died for you. He desires to forgive you and set you free from whatever sins you've committed against your children, or whatever you have done to your parents. He's offering you the kind of relationship that can change your life—if you'll only accept it.

CHAPTER SEVEN

Christian Dogs: The Commandment **AGAINST MURDER**

I have a friend who spent some time attending school deep in the American South. He lived a good distance from the campus, out in the country. When traveling on the road back and forth to school he always passed two old men, country farmers, whose house looked like something out of the depression era. These men were not friendly, never smiled, and pretty much kept to themselves. Most people were advised to just leave them alone, and because my friend was something of a city slicker he followed that advice.

The two men had a dog, a black and brown junkyard mutt that snarled, and growled, and barked at absolutely everybody and everything. Every day as my friend went past the house, the dog would chase his car and bark uncontrollably. Most of the time he just ignored the dog and kept on driving.

Then one weekend my friend took his bicycle out for a ride. When he pedaled past the house, the dog came out, growling and barking, and chased him just as he always did the car. Except that this time the dog managed to catch him, and bit him. My friend just quickly pedaled away, and got the bite treated at a local clinic, deciding not to pursue the matter with the owners. He did admit, however, that more than once, as he drove past the house, he was sorely tempted to get revenge by running over the nasty dog.

As it turns out he didn't have to. A few months later the dog just disappeared. Just like that, it was gone. A week or two after that, another dog appeared in its place. He assumed the old one had died. What was very interesting about the new dog was that, in the beginning, it didn't chase him. It just stood on the front lawn of the house and watched the cars go by. But then, over time, it started to act just like the first dog: barking, and snarling, and chasing the cars. Before long, he was just as mean and nasty as his predecessor.

Here's the question: Why did the second dog turn out just like the first one? Did those two old farmers just happen to walk into the pound and pick out two nasty dogs in a row? To be honest, I don't think so. I think the truth is that both dogs, in their own doggy way, started to reflect the meanness and nastiness of their owners. It's not that they purposely trained the dog to growl, and bark, and bite; I think the dogs, all on their own, started to pick up their owners' nasty attitudes. The only difference is that they took out their nastiness on passing cars.

There is some truth to this. Experienced veterinarians can tell a lot about the character, mood, and demeanor of dog owners they have never met when they observe the traits that are expressed in the dogs they own.

I know someone who worked on taking people's blood pressure readings in health vans that would drive through the city as a public service. Many of the people who worked in the van lived in a big mansion, which also functioned as the headquarters for their work. One day a new worker was hired who had a dog that he brought to the headquarters with him. Over time people started having a difficult time with this new guy, who was always angry, critical, judgmental, and just generally hard to get along with. One of his coworkers said, "I stay away from him because he doesn't have a Christian dog." It was true. The dog, in its own doggy way, also reflected the negativity, the hostility and nastiness of its owner.

The subject of this chapter is the sixth commandment, which simply says:

"You shall not murder." (Ex. 20:13)

Few people would dispute that the sixth commandment is still relevant for modern life. It seems that in spite of all our advances in the areas of science, culture and technology, murder is as big a problem as it's ever been. Somehow we're still killing each other just like we did back in less "civilized" times. In the late 1990s social commentator Richard John Neuhaus wrote: "In this century so many people have been deliberately killed by other people that the estimates of historians vary by the tens of millions, and they end up by agreeing to split the difference, or to round off the victim count at the nearest ten million."

Whether the Rwandan genocide, the Holocaust, the killing fields of Cambodia, Darfur, the Stalinist atrocities, whatever it is, the morbid list of mass murder in the twentieth century goes on, and on. Unfortunately, the new millennium isn't starting out too promising either. This century wasn't even two years old when 9/11 hit, when three thousand innocent men, woman, and children were murdered in one of the most brutal terrorist acts in modern history. The problem simply won't go away, and the value put on human life seems lower than ever.

That brings me to an important point. As we've been looking at the Ten Commandments, we've been doing it against the background of modern thought. Many people describe the period we live in, the postmodern era, as a time when the idea of objective truth has been dismissed as byproducts of the sterile coldness of the modern era. Now, instead of believing in absolute right or wrong, we think that codes of human behavior and morality are nothing more than human constructs—things we made up for ourselves—and we've come to the conclusion that nobody's code of conduct is better than somebody else's. At the end of the day, we've convinced ourselves that each one of us should set the rules for ourselves, and never pass judgment on someone else's moral code.

It's funny, but one expert in postmodern thought, Dr. Stanley J. Grenz, wrote tongue-in-cheek that: "Postmodernism was born in St. Louis, Missouri, on July 15, at 3:23 p.m." Why did he say that? That was the moment when some famous housing project, hailed as the epitome of "modernist architecture," or something like that, was razed to the ground by the city fathers, because the inhabitants had run it down so badly that it was no longer inhabitable. This demolition was deemed by some as the event that ended the modern era, and brought in the postmodern one.

I can't say I necessarily agree that this date was the beginning of the postmodern era: I don't really know when it began. But I know the date that it ended for many people—September 11, 2001. The cold-blooded and calculated slaughter of thousands of innocent people in broad daylight, broadcast on our television sets for everyone to watch, brought home for many people, in real time, the horror involved in murder. It was suddenly very obvious that evil like this could never be justified on the basis of culture.

This wasn't the cultural difference between someone's preference for croissants, and another's preference for English Muffins. On the day of 9/11 people saw the face of moral evil, an evil that transcends all cultures and traditions. Suddenly, the objective reality of evil, the real existence of morality, hit home for people as never before.

It seems all you need to do to prove the existence of real evil is to witness it practiced to the extreme. Even postmodernists can agree that murder is utterly wrong. You just can't justify it by appealing to cultural preference or ethnic diversity. In fact, most people don't even have to check the tables of stone to figure this out. We just know it's wrong.

That brings me back to the dogs. Jesus speaks on the subject of murder in Matthew chapter 5:

"You have heard that it was said to those of old, 'You shall not murder, and whoever murders will be in danger of the judgment.' But I say to you that whoever is angry with his brother without a cause shall be in danger of the judgment. And whoever says to his brother, 'Raca!' shall be in danger of the council. But whoever says, 'You fool!' shall be in danger of hell fire. Therefore if you bring your gift to the altar, and there remember that your brother has something against you, leave your gift there before the altar, and go your way. First be reconciled to your brother, and then come and offer your gift. Agree with your adversary quickly, while you are on the way with him, lest your adversary deliver you to the judge, the judge hand you over to the officer, and you be thrown into prison. Assuredly, I say to you, you will by no means get out of there till you have paid the last penny."
(Matthew 5:21-26)

Now, put aside the immediate cultural issues involved in this passage, and look at the principle that Jesus is stating. He unwraps this commandment in its deeper meaning for us. It's not just talking about the extreme act of physically killing someone. Jesus actually equates murder with some of our thoughts, feelings, and words. That's a whole new ball game. How in the world can your thoughts and words be the same thing as murder?

Let's go back to our dogs. The anger and bitterness felt by their owners was so obvious that even the dogs picked up on it and started to act it out. If that can happen with a bunch of dogs, what do you think happens when our anger and bitterness spill over onto other people?

All of us have a type of aura. Not the sort of wacky-colored force fields that psychics claim they can see around our heads, but the general atmosphere around us created by our emotions. We just can't help it; what percolates in our minds and hearts shows up on our face. It changes our demeanor, or words, and that can have a real impact on the people around us.

Jack grew up in a home where his father continually abused his mother and siblings, both physically and verbally. When Jack grew up, he did the same thing to *his* family. Is that a coincidence? Of course not, and Jack doesn't think so, either. He pretty much knows that it's ruining his wife and kids' lives.

You can imagine how much better it would have been if whatever made Jack's dad act that way had been nipped in the bud, before it started bearing such bitter fruit down through several generations. When you harbor resentment and hatred, it can have a devastating effect on people's lives for generations. And that's why Jesus warns us so strongly to reconcile with people now. Otherwise, your emotions might just eat you alive—and not just you, but also the people who live with you.

Just imagine what would happen if people actually dealt with anger before it expanded into violence. Imagine how much heartache we could avoid. Jesus tells us to uproot the early sentiments that eventually end in murder. He takes a commandment against killing, and paints a much bigger picture for us: one that includes important concepts like forgiveness, reconciliation, and healing. In a sense, Jesus is showing us that this commandment is not only for the benefit of would-be murder victims. It's also for the benefit of would-be murderers! He's trying to spare us the bitterness, the hatred, the suffering that comes from harboring bitter feelings that can lead to murder. Even then, it doesn't have to lead to murder to ruin your life.

A few centuries before Christ there lived a man named Fabius, who led Rome during one of the Punic Wars. Fabius learned that one of his officers was provoking discontent among the soldiers, even trying to get them to desert. Instead of torturing and killing the officer as was the usual treatment of rebellious soldiers, he called him in and talked with him. He asked the officer to bring his grievances to him instead of to others. At the end of the conversation he gave him a number of gifts, including an excellent horse. The result was an officer who became Fabius' most loyal soldier.

Jesus isn't just telling us not to commit murder. He's telling us to extinguish the thoughts, the anger, and the rage long before they turn into the act of murder. Just think about how much better you would feel if you could just let go of the anger and bitterness that's ruining your life, and that only differs from murder itself by a matter of degrees. Here's what Jesus is essentially saying: "Reconcile, reconcile, reconcile! Not just for the sake of your enemy, but for your sake, too."

Here's another good example from the history of the ancient Romans. A Carthaginian military leader was preparing for battle with the hated Romans when his son, a boy of ten, asked if he could go along. The father laughed him off, but the boy persistently pleaded. Finally the father stopped, grabbed the startled youngster, and carried him off to one of the temples where children were sacrificed to the Carthaginian gods. He held his boy over one of the fires that burned in the temple. Naturally the child was terrified. Was his dad really going to throw him into the flames?

Holding the boy over the fire the father shouted at him. "Son, do you swear eternal hatred to the Romans? Swear it, boy, swear it, or I will throw you in this fire!"

"Yes daddy, yes daddy. I swear, I swear."

"And you will fight the Romans to the day you die? Swear it, boy, swear it!"

"Yes daddy, I swear, I swear."

The father set the boy down, took him off to war, and when the father died years later, his son took over the army. That son was known as Hannibal, the man who for years caused havoc and bloodshed in Italy.

Eventually, furious at Hannibal's fifteen-year occupation, the Romans sailed to Carthage, burned all the Carthaginian ships in the harbor, and then went house to house murdering the occupants, taking those who survived into slavery.

I don't know for certain, because the Romans were hardly good neighbors, but maybe, just maybe, if the father had said to young Hannibal, "Let's try to reconcile with the Romans, son; let's try to be their friends—like brothers." If he had done that instead of filling the boy's heart with hatred, maybe that chapter of history might not have been so tragic.

Do you see my point? If we would only suppress the early sentiments, we could eliminate a lot of murder. But Jesus takes things even further. Not only does He tell us to stop killing, He also tells us to stop hating:

"You have heard that it was said, 'You shall love your neighbor and hate your enemy.' But I say to you, love your enemies, bless those who curse you, do good to those who hate you, and pray for those who spitefully use you and persecute you." (Matthew 5:43-44)

Try to wrap your mind around what Jesus said. It's one thing to tell us not to hate people who make us angry, and it's understandable to hear that we should reconcile with people who are at odds with us—but to tell us to love them? How in the world are we supposed to do that?

Uwe Boll is a German movie director who makes cheap films based on popular video games. His movies are considered the dregs: bad acting, mindless direction, with incomprehensible scripts. The on-line critics repeatedly skewered them. It got so bad that Boll, 41, a former boxer, full of rage and anger over what he deemed unfair treatment, made cinematic history, doing what, as far as I know, no director had ever done before. He challenged his critics to boxing matches.

Amazingly enough, the three worst offenders, the critics who hurt him the most, took up his challenge—and, one by one, he pummeled them into the ropes. He skewered them worse than they had his films. When it was over he grabbed a mike, and beaming from ear to ear shouted, "I hit them so hard they have brain damage. They love my movies now!"

I don't know about that, but I do know that Uwe Boll, at least for a few moments, was able to let off some of the rage and anger that was boiling up inside him. I really don't think it's going to last, though. I think he's going to need more than the temporary fix of pounding his fists into the faces of his critics to deal with his anger.

No doubt most of us need more than that, too. Who hasn't been hurt by life? Who hasn't felt rage, anger, or frustration at how people have treated us? I really doubt any have totally escaped those kinds of feelings. Maybe there are times when you've thought about pummeling the people who've hurt you. Let me tell you something I'm guessing you already know: that approach is not really going to solve the deeper issues going on inside of you.

Anger simply breeds more anger. Harbored resentment ruins not only your life, but also that of the people around you. Jesus is saying that He can fix the problem so completely that you not only stop hating people, you actually learn to love them. In His hand He's holding the keys that will set you free from years of life-crushing bitterness. Maybe you've allowed the people who've hurt you to keep on doing it because you're held prisoner by your hatred for them. But now you can experience freedom from that.

Jesus Himself, dying on the cross, suffering for the sins of the world, Jesus, who was treated so unfairly, so unjustly, had all the reasons in the world to be full of anger and bitterness. Yet, what did He say?

"... Father, forgive them, for they do not know what they do...." (Luke 23:34)

If you could, don't you think you'd rather have that kind of attitude? To give up hatred would change your life—and the lives of the people around you. Jesus knows full well what it means to have been ill-treated. He knows what it means to have faced injustice. He knows what it means to have been unfairly maligned and condemned. But He never allowed Himself to fall victim to the rage and hatred that these things can so easily cause. And because He is God, He can free you from the rage, the anger, and the bitterness that's inside your mind right now. All you need to do is give yourself to Him completely, accept that He forgives you and allow Him to control your thoughts and feelings.

Something remarkable happens when you see what God has done for you. You begin to believe that you can do the same for others. If God refuses to hate you, even after everything you've done—the times you've broken His laws, the times that you've shaken your fist at heaven when it wasn't God's fault, the times that you hurt one of His children—if God can forgive you for that, then maybe you can start forgiving other people. After all, your hatred is not only killing them, it's killing you, too.

No question, the world is full of hate, so much so that even people's dogs reflect it. But you don't have to be that way. Believe me, you can rise above it with Jesus.

CHAPTER EIGHT

The Sad Saga of **JACK**

This is the story of a man we'll call Jack. Jack married Stephanie, his high school sweetheart, the day after graduation. They joked about how Stephanie took off her graduation gown to put on a wedding gown. In their second year of college, Stephanie found herself pregnant, and quit school. By the time Jack graduated, two more babies had arrived. Jack got a good job with good pay, allowing Stephanie to stay at home with the children, which was just fine with her.

On the outside they looked like a healthy, happy, loving couple with three wonderful children. There was just one problem. Her name was Jan, and she worked in Jack's office. She was younger than Stephanie by eight years, and since she hadn't had any children, she was built more to Jack's ideal than Stephanie now was. Besides that, she was always well-dressed and sharp looking, in striking contrast to Stephanie, who after a long day of dealing with three kids, hardly looked like a beauty queen. On top of that, Jan was always full of life. Most amazing of all, she loved hockey, something that was Jack's passion and which Stephanie hated. In fact, every time Jack tried to watch hockey at home, Stephanie tried to get him to turn it off.

Over time Jack felt his emotions—not to mention his passions—getting out of control. He was becoming obsessed with Jan, who not only knew it, but also went out of her way to dress provocatively to get his attention. Over and over, Jack would mentally wander into dangerous territory, and then quickly pull back, telling himself, "this is wrong!"

One day, as Jack was driving his car listening to an oldies station, a song came on about a married man who fell in love with another woman, saying, "If loving you is wrong, I don't wanna be right." Well, that was it. Jack told Jan he loved her, and they both left work early the next day—if you get my drift.

It isn't rocket science to figure out what happened next. Jack and Stephanie's marriage fell apart, he married Jan, and life went on. But it didn't go on quite like before. Jack's kids, angry about the divorce, became difficult to handle, especially the oldest boy, who already had a drug habit by the age of fourteen. Stephanie was forced to work, and between the stresses of single motherhood and trying to earn a living, she collapsed with a nervous breakdown that landed her in the hospital.

Unfortunately, she didn't have any insurance, which made things even tougher. Finally, the ten-year-old girl went to stay with an aunt and uncle, where it was later discovered that the uncle was abusing her.

But that's only Stephanie's side of the story. The honeymoon with Jack and Jan didn't last long, either. First of all, Stephanie "took him to the cleaners" for child support, which forced him to find extra work, and which kept him away from Jan a lot more than he wanted. The kids hated Jan with a passion, so when they came to stay with Jack they made her life an absolute nightmare. Over time, with Jack away at work so much, Jan started seeing another man, and inside of a couple of years, she left Jack.

Devastated by all these events Jack couldn't concentrate on his work, and lost his job. That was something that would have happened anyway, because all the time, behind the scenes, it turns out that Jan was working hard to get him fired. Because he was way behind in his child support, Jack was dragged into court, and faced the prospect of jail time if he didn't pay up.

It's an ugly end to a really sad story. Last I heard, Stephanie was living in poverty, using food stamps and other forms of welfare, somewhere in greater Los Angeles. The oldest boy, now sixteen, dropped out of school and wound up in a drug rehab center, and the daughter, now fifteen, wound up pregnant and got the idea that she and Stephanie could raise the baby together. And Jack? Well, he ended up holding down two dead-end jobs and developing a taste for gin and tonic.

All this tragedy—for what? For lust? For passion? A family is utterly destroyed and lives are ruined. I guarantee you, when Jack visits his sixteen-year-old son in rehab or his single-mom fifteen-year-old daughter, I'll bet he doesn't think it's worth it.

It reminds me of a story that somebody wrote a few years ago about a teenager who committed suicide by drinking Nestlé's chocolate laced with cyanide. When the father walked into the room, he saw his boy on the floor, and tried to revive him with mouth-to-mouth resuscitation. The only problem with that was that the father got cyanide on his own lips, and ended up dying too. Then the mother walked into the room, saw her husband on the floor, and did the same thing. After that, the daughter came in, and repeated the process. Before it was over, the whole family was dead.

Of course, this never actually happened. But the story, although a little silly, does makes an important point. When you decide to do something wrong, it almost always has an impact on others; usually those who are the closest to you, the ones you love the most. Nowhere is this more obvious than in the area of marital infidelity—which is why God has drawn some very clear boundaries around the sacred institution of marriage. In fact, He literally wrote those boundaries in stone, in the Ten Commandments. Point blank He tells us:

"You shall not commit adultery." (Exodus 20:14)

There's a very good reason God told us not to commit adultery. That reason is because He has our best interests at heart. If anything proves that God loves to give us good things, it's the arrangement He created for marriage and family. If you really think about it, He could have provided any one of a thousand different ways for babies to make their entrance into this world without making it an emotionally and physically pleasing experience. He could have made the whole process no more complicated than scratching an itch, or some other sort of thoughtless mechanism. We still would have filled the earth with offspring, but that's not the model He gave us. You've got to admit that the marriage relationship is for more than simple procreation. It adds levels of intimacy, passion, and love that clearly demonstrate a God who wanted to give us a wonderful gift.

Of course, what some people will say is that it's not always wonderful. In fact, in some people's experience it's a huge source of misery and suffering. If it's really a gift from God, then why does it turn out wrong so much of the time? Frankly, the answer's pretty easy: it's because we've abused the gift.

Let me see if I can illustrate this. Adolph Hitler was one of the greatest orators of the twentieth century, but he used his remarkable gift to curse the world. He got his start at the end of World War I, when small, bitter, political groups would meet in the taverns and beer halls of Weimar, Germany to commiserate about losing the war. Hitler got involved in one of these groups, a marginal band of thugs called the National Socialists. This group probably would have faded into nothing, except for the fact that Hitler started to speak at their meetings with his gift for mesmerizing an audience. Over time, so many people came under his spell that not only did he rise to the top of the party, but he also dragged the whole nation in his wake. If Hitler had stammered or mumbled, the whole world would have been a different place.

Let me ask you an easy question: Just because Hitler abused the gift of motivational speech, does that make public speaking in and of itself an evil thing? Of course not. From Billy Graham to Winston Churchill, lots of people have used it wisely. The problem isn't with the gift; it's what you do with it.

The same is true for human sexuality. It's a wonderful gift, but as the author of that gift, God knows full well it can be abused. That's why He puts a deliberate fence around it, to spare us the pain. It's the seventh commandment:

"You shall not commit adultery." (Exodus 20:14)

I can't begin to tell you about all the ruined lives and marriages caused by breaking this one commandment. But I'm also pretty sure I don't need to, because I'm guessing you've already seen what it does to other people, or maybe even had your own life damaged by it.

Not too long ago, a young woman, about twenty-five years old, talked to a group of young people about her parents' divorce; a divorce all because the mother had found a new boyfriend. As this young woman, now married and with a baby of her own, talked about the divorce, which had happened more than fifteen years before, you could hear the pain and devastation in her voice. The event was still haunting her. Here she was, an innocent victim, suffering the consequences of someone else's violation of the seventh commandment. She's been scarred for life because of her mother's choice to break her marriage vow.

I wonder, how many homes, how many marriages, how many childhoods have been destroyed by this action? How much pain might have been spared, how many homes kept intact, how many lives would be richer and fuller if people lived within God's boundaries?

If you've been thinking about adultery as a way out, I can promise you—beyond the shadow of a doubt—that you're wrong. I promise that if you go through with it, whatever pleasure you stand to gain will be offset a thousand fold by the suffering that will surely follow.

When Ronald Reagan was president, he said something I believe was pretty smart. Something to the effect of: "If you want to stay a happy man, never cheat on your wife." I couldn't agree more.

In spite of what some people have been saying, God is not opposed to sexuality; in fact, it was His idea in the first place. He made it for humans to enjoy. But it is to be experienced within the boundary He created, because He knows this boundary forms an important wall of protection. The boundary is remarkably simple: sexual relationships are for a man and a woman inside the bonds of marriage. Outside of that arrangement, according to the Bible, you are abusing the gift, and that abuse can bring untold pain and suffering.

In case you still don't believe it, just think about it. Ask any one of the millions of unwed girls who got pregnant as teenagers if they wish they had obeyed that commandment. Ask any one of the men and women suffering from sexually transmitted diseases, especially the women left barren by the disease, or ask anyone who got AIDS in adultery if they wish they had kept the commandment. Ask any one of the millions of children whose childhoods are ruined because of adultery—just ask them if they wish their parents had kept the commandment. The human toll caused by this particular sin is something I'm pretty sure we'll never accurately calculate. Back in 1970, at the height of what was called the "sexual revolution," *Life* magazine ran an article that said, "In the first place, we must rid our minds of the idea that there are any special moral rules for sexual behavior. Sexual pleasure is never wrong."

Never wrong? Are you kidding? Try telling that to Jack's kids, or to the young woman who's never going to have kids because of the disease she got from a casual encounter. Try reading that statement to someone dying from AIDS because they chose to have an affair? Is it *really* never wrong? Of course not, and Western civilization is starting to wake up to what God has said all along: sex outside of marriage is always wrong. But in a world that's let go of the moral values that held our civilization together for thousands of years, some people still struggle to figure out why this statement is true.

Someone once asked a preacher why sex outside of marriage is wrong. He pointed out the window to a well-manicured lawn and said, "It's beautiful, isn't it?"

"Yes, preacher, it really is!"

"Well," said the preacher, "if I took that same lawn and put it on your living room floor, it would turn into nothing but dirt, wouldn't it?"

He's exactly right. God wants you to have something beautiful. He wants you to have the joy, the bliss, and wonderment of an intimate physical relationship—not the loss and devastation that comes from abusing it. In fact, far from what some people might have you believe, God wants you to enjoy your sexuality greatly. Read what the Apostle Paul says when he talks about husbands and wives:

Nevertheless, because of sexual immorality, let each man have his own wife, and let each woman have her own husband. Let the husband render to his wife the affection due her, and likewise also the wife to her husband. The wife does not have authority over her own body, but the husband does. And likewise the husband does not have authority over his own body, but the wife does. Do not deprive one another except with consent for a time, that you may give yourselves to fasting and prayer; and come together again so that Satan does not tempt you because of your lack of self-control.
(1 Corinthians 7:2-5)

It's not me telling you to enjoy your married relationship more; it's the Bible. It is basically telling married folks not to deprive each other. And when it comes to overdoing it, the only warning given is to avoid too much *abstinence!* You'll never convince me that the Bible or Christianity is prudish or repressed. I mean, please—have you ever read the Song of Solomon? In the right context, the context of Godly marriage, the Bible shows us a path to sexual fulfillment you'll never find somewhere else.

Maybe you've read some of the studies done on sexual satisfaction. It turns out that married couples who stay faithful to each other report higher sexual satisfaction than those who practice sex outside of marriage; that practicing sex within the safety and security of marriage is actually more satisfying than running around with a number of different partners. That's what God's been trying to say all along: a married man will find more fulfillment with his wife than with a one-night stand picked up at a bar.

Henry Ford and his wife were celebrating their fiftieth wedding anniversary when someone asked him the secret of his marital success. Ford responded, "The formula is the same as I used to make a successful car: Stick to one model."

Millions of people can tell you he was right. Of course, sexual temptation can be pretty powerful. But it's that very power that gives a godly relationship the potential for so much intimacy, closeness, and love. Only those who have experienced the wonder and the beauty of sexual love within the bounds that God created will know how fulfilling it can really be. And those who step outside of those bounds can tell you how much pain and suffering it causes. Just ask Jack; or Stephanie; or their kids.

When interpreting this commandment, Jesus said:

"You have heard that it was said to those of old, 'You shall not commit adultery.' But I say to you that whoever looks at a woman to lust for her has already committed adultery with her in his heart." (Matthew 5:27-28)

Did you see that? *Lust in your heart is the same as adultery.* Jesus knows how powerful the sexual drive can be, and He also knows how devastating its abuse can be. So He is telling us to nip it in the bud. Deal with the problem at the level where it always begins:

in your mind. Take care of it before it moves into your real life where you're going to have a lot more trouble controlling it. If Jack had just listened to what Jesus said, if millions of people had just stopped the lust before it turned to adultery, how much better their lives would be today.

Try to imagine a world where sex was always practiced within the boundaries that God created. Be honest: take away the values used in the Playboy mansion, and ask yourself if the world would be better or worse. The answer is obvious, of course, because as it turns out, God is always right.

Perhaps you're thinking it's too late. You've blown it, and more than once. But the news from the Bible is good: it's never too late to do the right thing. In fact, in one of the most famous stories in the Bible (found in John 8), a woman caught in the act of adultery is brought to Jesus, and He forgives her—just like that. That same Jesus is willing to forgive you too. No matter what you've done, no matter how much pain you've caused, no matter what you're going through, you can be forgiven. It's possible, because Jesus suffered the results of your sin on the cross and paid the price for what you did, in full. You just need to confess, repent and claim the promise for Him to forgive and cleanse you.

Believe me, it's never too late. The Bible not only promises that you can have forgiveness, it also says that you can have healing. You can have the power to live a better kind of life. You can live without being a slave to your passions. But, it's not me making you that promise, it's God, in the pages of His book.

So let me ask you: What in the world are you waiting for?

CHAPTER NINE

Victims, Villains and Hardly **ANY HEROES**

On January 25, 2005, Cliff quietly got of bed, being careful not to disturb his wife who was sleeping soundly next to him in their huge suburban home outside of Houston, Texas. Staying quiet, so as not to waken his two sleeping children, he left the house and drove off in his brand new Mercedes S500.

Cliff was obviously wealthy. As a corporate executive in the oil industry, he had a fancy home, fancy cars, and even owned a seventy-two foot yacht called the *Tranquility Base.* This Long Island policeman's son was a millionaire many times over. Most important of all, he came by it honestly and fairly, because Cliff was not a crook.

So how was it that Cliff suddenly found himself immersed in all sorts of legal investigations? The FBI and the SEC were involved, as well as the United States Congress, as he was dragged into a massive securities fraud investigation. He was convinced that agents were tailing him, and rummaging through his trash. And even though nobody believed that Cliff was involved in the criminal activities which led to the downfall of America's seventh-largest company, there was no way he could escape the stigma.

No doubt Cliff was taking it pretty hard. The sleeping pills and anti-depressants were supposed to help, but they only seemed to make matters worse. No one will ever know for sure exactly what was in his mind that night, but it couldn't have been good; because even though we're reasonably certain he did nothing wrong, he parked his car in the middle of the street, locked the doors, pulled out his .357 revolver, and ended it all—at least for himself.

John Clifford Baxter, age 43, became another tragic victim in a situation that has produced almost nothing but victims: victims, and villains, with hardly any heroes. We're talking about the Enron collapse, the demise of a company that declared 111 billion dollars in assets in 2000, but declared bankruptcy by the end of 2001. It was the second largest bankruptcy in the history of America, a bankruptcy that ruined thousands of lives, sent some of America's top corporate talent to jail, destroyed the famous Arthur Anderson auditing firm, and led to the demise of one of the nation's most innovative and powerful companies. How did it happen, and what can we learn from it?

I'm not here to judge anyone, and certainly not the men involved in the Enron fiasco. The courts have already done that. But courts of law can't judge the human heart: actions, yes, perceived motives, yes, results, yes, but the innermost thoughts, feelings, and reasons of the heart, no. The courts can't do that, and neither can I.

Blaise Pascal, the famous philosopher, once said: "The heart has reasons that reason can never know." He's absolutely right. I don't know the hearts of the Enron executives, I don't know the deepest reasons for their actions—and really, I don't need to. The Bible teaches that one day God "...will both bring to light the hidden things of darkness and reveal the counsels [or motives] of the hearts" (1 Corinthians 4:5).

On that day the real truth is going to surface: for the Enron executives, and for all the rest of us. We must be careful that we don't sit as judges, because Jesus Himself once said:

"Judge not, and you shall not be judged." (Luke 6:37)

Nevertheless, if we ever needed an example of how our violation of God's law can bring ruin upon ourselves and others, we have it right here in the sad story of Enron.

In studying the Ten Commandments so far, we've discovered that while keeping the commandments will never buy your way out of your sin and guilt, or pay for your sins, God still expects us to live by them. The Bible's teaching on the purpose of the law is crystal clear; it doesn't make up for your sins, and it doesn't buy you a ticket to heaven. Here's what it says in Galatians chapter two:

...knowing that a man is not justified by the works of the law, but by faith in Jesus Christ, even we have believed in Jesus Christ, that we might be justified by the faith of Christ, and not by the works of the law: for by the works of the law shall no flesh be justified. (Galatians 2:16)

It really couldn't be any clearer than that. You just can't keep enough of the law to buy yourself a spot in heaven, and make up for the laws you've already broken. But the Bible is also clear that God gives us His law because He loves us and wants the best for us. On top of that, the Bible also teaches that keeping God's law really isn't much of a burden, not if you take to heart what it says in 1 John 5:3:

For this is the love of God, that we keep His commandments: and His commandments are not burdensome. (1 John 5:3)

If you ever wanted to see the value, the practical importance of keeping God's commandments, you have it in the story of Enron. Maybe you've heard the statement that a conservative is a liberal who's been mugged. Let me modify that a little bit. A moral absolutist is a postmodernist who's been robbed. What does that mean? Well, a postmodernist, at least in part, is someone who believes that there is no such thing as absolute right and wrong. He believes that everyone has the right to determine what is right and wrong for himself without outside interference. Everyone has his or her own set of moral values, and no one has the right to judge another person, because no one can see things clearly anyway.

Personally, I've met people who claim to believe that very concept. But I suspect that if you pressed them hard, you'll find out they don't *really* believe it. And for sure I know that the thousands of folks at Enron who lost their income, health insurance, and retirement savings don't believe it, either. Somehow, when somebody else breaks God's law, we automatically know it still applies.

I don't pretend to understand all of the sordid details in the Enron case; the shenanigans that led to an estimated loss of about fifty billion dollars. It took federal and state investigators years to sort it all out, especially after Enron's auditing firm started destroying documents. But this much I do know: a violation of the eighth commandment led to a tragedy of gargantuan proportions.

On the surface Enron seemed like it would have been a great place to work. People like Henry Kissinger, and former Secretary of State James Baker had served on the board. Nobel Laureate Nelson Mandela flew in from Africa to receive the Enron Prize. And President George W. Bush famously referred to the Enron founder and chairman, as "Kenny Boy." It was hailed in newspapers and magazines as a model company, a pioneer paving the way to a new millennium of business opportunities.

It seemed like an honest business, too. Notice these words from Enron's 1998 annual report, just three years before the collapse. "We treat others as we would like to be treated ourselves. … We will work with customers and prospects openly, honestly and sincerely."

That sounds pretty good. But the truth is, as the company was going bust, its executives were telling investors and workers that everything was great, that there was no need to panic, and that their investments were secure—even though those same executives were selling their own shares and pocketing millions of dollars in the process. The worst part may have been that almost every dollar was taken out of the retirement plans of the workers!

That's hardly "treating others as they'd like to be treated themselves." In fact, it's more like the passage found in James chapter 5:

Come now, you rich, weep and howl for your miseries that are coming upon you! Your riches are corrupted, and your garments are moth-eaten. Your gold and silver are corroded, and their corrosion will be a witness against you and will eat your flesh like fire. You have heaped up treasure in the last days. Indeed the wages of the laborers who mowed your fields, which you kept back by fraud, cry out;...(James 5:1-4)

Through crooked accounting practices, insider trading, deceit and lies, the leaders of Enron were covering up the fact that the company was losing billions of dollars. They did this in order to keep the stock price high to reap their multi-million dollar bonuses every year, as well as sell their stocks at inflated prices. And what made matters worse was the fact that when stocks started falling, company executives didn't allow workers to sell their shares, even though that's what they were doing themselves.

Let's take a look at one striking example. One of Enron's two top executives, Jeffrey Skilling, was taking in tens of millions (at one point even selling seventy million dollars worth of shares) while thousands of employees—who believed Skilling's words that the company was doing fine—watched their own pension plans crash when Enron stock collapsed from a high of ninety dollars a share down to sixty-one cents.

Skilling was eventually sentenced to more than twenty-four years in prison where he'll make anywhere from about twelve cents an hour to, if he's really lucky, about $1.25 an hour. He's going to have to make a lot more than that, however, if he ever hopes to settle the millions of dollars in civil suits that have been filed against him. Andrew Fastow, the chief financial officer and the brains behind some of Enron's shadiest deals, got seven years, but that was only after he ratted on the others. And then there was Kenneth Lay, who declared his innocence up until the end, even after selling stocks and pocketing tens of millions, even after his conviction on twenty-nine criminal counts, including conspiracy and fraud, and facing up to forty-five years in prison.

"Certainly this is not the outcome we expected," Lay said after his conviction. "I firmly believe I am innocent of the charges against me, as I have said from day one." Lay never made it through his sentencing. He died of a heart attack shortly after the conviction.

Only God can sort out everything that really happened, and who was really guilty. But if you need an example of how selfishness and sin can hurt a lot of people, the collapse of Enron paints a pretty clear picture.

Try to imagine the situation. You've been working for years at a company. You give your life to it. And though you hear rumors that things are going bad, and your retirement portfolio is shrinking because the company's stock is falling, the chief executives keep telling you everything is okay, not to worry, the company is in great shape, better than ever in fact, and that before long things will be back to normal.

To make matters worse, they won't allow you to sell your stock. Then, when you come back to work one day, you are told to clear out your desk, because you no longer have a job. Everything is gone: your paycheck, your company health insurance, and, the worst of it is, your retirement portfolio that you built up for years has dwindled down to nothing. Multiply that scenario by thousands, and you'll begin to understand the massive suffering and loss that happened at Enron. It all happened because somebody chose to break the eighth commandment, the one that plainly says, "You shall not steal."

You see, whether it's robbing a bank at gunpoint, or cooking the books at Enron, in God's eyes, it's all the same thing: it's stealing. Of course, not all thievery comes with the vast consequences of the

Enron debacle, and stealing doesn't have to be in the millions of dollars to have terrible consequences, does it?

I have some friends who had a small generator sitting in their garage, which they bought in anticipation of the Y2K crisis. One afternoon they left the garage door open, and someone came in and stole it. It was only a generator, and insurance covered the theft, but greater than the material loss was a sense of having been violated. There's something "sacred" about ownership, about having some things that are yours, that belong to only you.

Over a hundred years ago Karl Marx ranted and raved about the evils of private property, as if it were the cause of all our problems on earth. We know firsthand how well his theory turned out, however. There's something very basic, very human, about private ownership. It's just part of who we are as human beings, at least in a sinful world.

So when you're the victim of theft—whether it's corporate fraud, or a pickpocket—there's a sense that something basic to your humanity has been violated. Your very personhood, your personal space, has been desecrated, and as anyone who has ever been robbed can tell you, it's a very uncomfortable feeling.

There's another reason why we've been given the commandment against stealing. It might surprise you, but I think this commandment is just as much to protect the thief as it is the victim. Let me try to explain.

Alexander grew up in a very dysfunctional home with a single mom, an absentee father, and was involved with a rough group of friends. At seventeen, Alexander saw a car idling in front of a Starbucks, and on a whim jumped in the car, a Lexus SUV, and gunned it.

After a few minutes of driving the stolen car, when his heart had stopped racing, and the intensity of the actual theft started to wear off, he was horrified. *How could I have done this?* he thought. More than once he was ready to pull over, jump out, and run. But he kept on driving, and with each passing mile the sense of the seriousness of his crime grew less and less acute. The longer he drove, the less guilty he felt. Later he said that after about two hours he no longer thought he had done anything wrong. On the contrary, he actually started thinking the car was his!

I see this as a vivid example of what happens to us when we commit any kind of sin, but especially something as blatant as stealing. After all, who really needs a commandment to know that stealing is wrong? It's all but written on the walls of our conscience. Add to that what society says and what God's law says, and people simply have no excuse. If they're going to steal, they have to violate their conscience to do it.

But each time they do it, it gets easier and easier, as if the writing on the wall gets a little more blurred with each successive theft. They learn to ignore the cries of their conscience until those cries become nothing but a whisper. Then they begin to ignore their conscience in other areas too, and before long they find themselves doing things that would have horrified them a few years before.

There's a text in the Bible where the Apostle Paul is talking about the difference between a mature Christian, someone who can eat meat, as opposed to someone who is immature, and who can only drink milk:

For though by this time you ought to be teachers, you need someone to teach you again the first principles of the oracles of God; and you have come to need milk and not solid food. For everyone who partakes only of milk is unskilled in the word of righteousness, for he is a babe. But solid food belongs to those who are of full age, that is, those who by reason of use have their senses exercised to discern both good and evil. (Hebrews 5:12-14)

Don't miss this point. We're supposed to learn to distinguish between good and evil. How? By "reason of use," by the constant practice of discerning between right and wrong, and between good and evil, by constantly making the choice to do what is right as opposed to what is wrong. That is how we learn to better understand the difference between the two. In contrast then, what surer way to get hardened in evil than to keep on doing it?

You've probably heard the story of putting a frog in a pot of steaming hot water, and it quickly jumps out. That just makes sense. So what do you do if you want to boil the frog alive? You place him in a pot of cool water, and then you slowly warm it. The frog gradually becomes acclimated to the water as it gets warmer and warmer, and just sits there, enjoying its bath until it's boiled alive.

The lesson, of course, is obvious. Sin does the same thing to our hearts. The more you do it, the more you like it; and the more you like it, the less wrong it feels. Until one day it no longer feels wrong at all. And that's just the danger. If we keep saying "yes" to sin, eventually it doesn't feel like sin anymore, it just feels like the natural thing to do, or perhaps may even feel like the *right* thing to do. And at that point, we've lost our ability to discern. The Bible warns us of this danger.

Woe to those who call evil good, and good evil; Who put darkness for light, and light for darkness. (Isaiah 5:20)

The best thing to do when faced with temptation and sin is to just say "no." God has promised that you'll never be faced with a temptation that you and He can't handle.

No temptation has overtaken you except such as is common to man; but God is faithful, who will not allow you to be tempted beyond what you are able, but with the temptation will also make the way of escape, that you may be able to bear it. (1 Corinthians 10:13)

You can claim the promise that in Jesus you can have the power to resist the temptation. God has given you permission to say "no" to sin. And if you do that consistently, eventually that sin which seemed so much fun, or gave you so much pleasure, will simply have lost its appeal. Rather than loving sin you will come to hate it. Instead you will exclaim, "Oh, how I love Your law" just like David did in Psalm 119:97. Listen to what he says later on in that same chapter:

Great peace have those who love Your law, and nothing causes them to stumble. (Psalm 119:165)

When we sin we have no peace, but when we learn to love God's law, not only do we have peace but according to this Bible promise, we also won't stumble.

Now, perhaps you've been a thief. Remember, not all thieves wear masks, climb walls at night, or hold up convenience stores with shotguns. Not all thieves "cook the books" as at Enron. Thievery can be a lot more subtle than all that.

There are a thousand ways to be a thief, a thousand ways to steal, but there is only one way to find peace and forgiveness with God, and that's through Jesus. No matter what you've done, you can at this moment be forgiven by God, if you will but ask Him for forgiveness. You can go to Jesus and ask him to take your sins away because that's the reason he came.

And you know that He was manifested to take away our sins.... (1 John 3:5)

Along with that, you can also go to Jesus and claim the promise of a new life, and a new heart. You see, the gospel isn't just about forgiveness, it's also about restoration. You can be free from this sin, this crime—you really can. Jesus has promised us:

"Therefore if the Son makes you free, you shall be free indeed." (John 8:36)

I don't have to tell you that stealing is wrong. It's not just a sin, it's a crime. You don't need the Bible to tell you that. What you do need to know, however, is where you can find forgiveness, healing, and a chance to start over. You can find it at the foot of the cross where you can look up and see and innocent Savior suffering the results of your sins. That's how much he loves you. And by doing that, he gives you a chance to begin again. Won't you accept his gracious offer?

What keeps you from doing the right thing, right now? Do it while you can still hear Jesus, loud and clear, saying to you:

"Behold, I stand at the door and knock. If anyone hears My voice and opens the door, I will come in to him and dine with him, and he with Me." (Revelation 3:20)

Let me put it this way: Better to have Jesus knocking at the door, instead of the police—wouldn't you say?

CHAPTER TEN

Lies and the Lying LIARS WHO TELL THEM

The year was 1944. The United States was in the midst of World War II, a war against the Japanese in the Pacific, and the Germans in the East. I don't think I'm exaggerating when I say that the fate of civilization literally hung in the balance. Just try to imagine how different our world would be if the Allies had lost. The American president at the time was Franklin D. Roosevelt, and as commander-in-chief of the United States military, Roosevelt had to be at the top of his game. That is precisely what the American people saw: a jaunty and robust leader inspiring the nation during its darkest hour. Roosevelt and his team used every means available to let the American people know that he was in the best of health and up to the heavy tasks and awesome responsibilities that fell on him. When asked by reporters about Roosevelt's health, Harry Truman, who had just finished lunch with the president, assured them that Roosevelt, "Looked great, and ate a bigger lunch than I did."

There was only one small problem. Everybody was lying. Roosevelt lied. His doctors lied. His cabinet lied. Even Truman lied;

something that's evident in a statement he made to Harry Vaughn about the very same lunch, saying, "I'd had no idea he was in such a feeble condition."

The entire administration was lying, because, far from being healthy, Roosevelt was dying. He had acute bronchitis, hypertension, hypertensive heart disease, and cardiac failure. In 1944, the year before his death, Roosevelt's blood pressure numbers were as high as 186/108, 200/108, 210/112, and 260/150. You don't have to be a doctor to know how bad those readings really are. Because of the president's congestive heart failure, he couldn't even breathe when he was lying down, and for months he had been sleeping with four-inch blocks of wood propping up the head of the bed in order to keep his head elevated enough so he wouldn't suffocate. Someone who had seen him said, "The president was the worst-looking man I ever saw who was still alive."

The commander-in-chief was so sick some days that he only worked four hours, and on other days he could manage only two. On the morning of April 12, 1945, Roosevelt put on a dark-gray suit and red tie to pose for a watercolor portrait. As the artist painted, Roosevelt lit a cigarette, raised his left hand to his temple, and squeezed his forehead, uttering his famous last words: "I have a terrific headache." Then he keeled over, and two hours later, the man who everyone said was the paragon of health, died from a massive stroke.

Okay, they all lied. But this was war, right? After all, we were fighting the Nazis. And, maybe, just maybe, if our government hadn't lied, we'd all be speaking German or Japanese. Didn't Churchill once say something to the effect of, "In wartime, truth is so precious that she should always be attended to by a bodyguard of lies"?

Besides, this wasn't a president lying under oath about his promiscuity, or covering up for Watergate. It wasn't even one well-known vice president telling people that his mother used to lull him to sleep as a baby with the song, "Look for the Union Label," even though it wasn't written until he was twenty-seven years old!

No, this was different, right? This was lying for the good of the country, for the fate of the free world. Well, fair enough. I know that the issue of lying can get pretty complex, and I've studied enough situation ethics to know about the grey areas in life and choosing the lesser of two evils. But I still want to draw your attention to the Bible, in particular to the ninth commandment, where God says:

"You shall not bear false witness against your neighbor." (Exodus 20:16)

Just in case we're tempted to think that God is only talking about neighbors, don't forget this passage in the book of Revelation, chapter 21:

"But the cowardly, unbelieving, abominable, murderers, sexually immoral, sorcerers, idolaters, and all liars shall have their part in the lake which burns with fire and brimstone, which is the second death." (Revelation 21:8)

I hope you noticed that it said "*all* liars." It didn't limit things to just lying about your neighbor. Couple that with a statement Jesus made about liars back in His day:

"You are of your father the devil, and the desires of your father you want to do. He was a murderer from the beginning, and does not stand in the truth, because there is no truth in him. When he speaks a lie, he speaks from his own resources, for he is a liar and the father of it." (John 8:44)

Now, those are pretty tough words. According to Jesus, the devil is not only a liar, but also the father of lies. And if the devil is the father of lies, and we lie—well, I think you get my drift. To put things mildly, the Bible treats the sin of lying in pretty clear-cut terms. Of all the commandments we've looked at so far, this is the first one that deals strictly with our words. All the others deal with our actions; how we act in relation to God and our fellow human beings. But this commandment takes morality to a deeper level, to the level of what we say.

There's a story in the Talmud (an ancient Jewish commentary on the Bible) where a king was entertained by two witty court jesters. One day, in a philosophical mood, the king tells one jester, "Simon, go out and bring back the best thing in all the world." Then he tells the other jester, "John, go out and bring back the worst thing in all the world." So the two of them depart. When they return, they stand in front of the king, each holding a little packet. Simon opens his and reveals what he believes is the best thing in the world: it's a tongue! Laughing, John comes forward and opens his packet, which is supposed to contain the worst thing in the world. His package has in it a tongue, too.

We shouldn't miss the point: the gift of speech is one of the most wonderful gifts God has given us—but it can also be one of the most abused, with the potential of doing incredible damage. (Just read James 3:5-7). One of the most obvious ways we abuse the gift of speech is through the sin of lying.

I find it strange that in our postmodern world, where nobody believes in absolute right and wrong, calling someone a liar is still one of the worst things you can say about them. Nobody wants to be called a liar. Some years ago, political comedian Al Franken put out a book called *Lies and the Lying Liars Who Tell Them: A Fair and Balanced Look at the Right*, hardly a subtle title, but one which makes a point. Even though the world is telling us that right and wrong aren't absolute anymore, we still instinctively know that lying is wrong.

A lot of people have the secular atheistic view of the world that teaches that our existence began with pure chance, the accidental mixing of elements and chemicals that kicked off the process of evolution. Now, if this was really true, and if we really were the products of accidental forces, then you'd have to ask the question, "What's wrong with lying or deception if it helps you survive?"

Far from being immoral, lying in order to take care of yourself would, in my humble opinion, seem to fall right in harmony with "the survival of the fittest." But here's the thing that doesn't fit: there are a lot of secular, postmodern people who believe in evolution, but still don't believe in telling lies. For some reason, they suffer a twinge of guilt when they lie. Why is that? How does that fit in with the evolutionary model?

Frankly, it doesn't. The truth is, we are moral beings created by a moral God who has given us a conscience. That conscience tells us that lying is wrong, that it causes problems. The Word of God speaks strongly against lying, and is filled with examples of lying and the troubles it brings.

You barely flip the first page in the Bible and you come to the story of Eve in the Garden of Eden with the lying serpent. God told Adam and Eve that if they ate from the forbidden tree they would surely die. But Satan, "the father of lies" as Jesus called him, said, "You shall not surely die" (Genesis 3:4).

God says one thing, and Satan says another. Then, practically on the same page, we have Cain, who just murdered his brother, lying to God:

Then the LORD said to Cain, "Where is Abel your brother?" He said, "I do not know. Am I my brother's keeper?" (Genesis 4:9)

That was an outright lie, and right to God's face. And what about the horrible deception that Jacob played on his old blind father, lying right to his face about which son he was, and stealing the blessing that belonged to his brother Esau? In the end that lie caused pain and suffering for the whole family.

Then there's the story of Joseph, who was sold into slavery by his brothers. They took his coat, dipped it in animal blood, and made their poor old father believe his son was killed by a wild animal. That caused deep pain and suffering for years. Later in Egypt, Joseph was thrown in prison because of the lies of his master's wife who tried to seduce him. And Sarah lied when she said she hadn't laughed at the promise of God. All this, in just the first book of the Old Testament!

Skip over to the New Testament and you find the same thing again. The Roman guards lied about what happened at the tomb of Jesus, and the religious leaders lied about Jesus as well. Ananias and Sapphira lied about the money they had given to the church. Peter lied when he denied Jesus—and he did it three times! All through the Bible, in the Old Testament and the New Testament, we are given scores of striking examples of people who lied and the problems these lies caused.

No one likes to be lied to, either. It makes you feel like a fool: violated, cheated and deceived. It's a terrible feeling. No wonder the Psalmist wrote: "Deliver my soul, O LORD, from lying lips And from a deceitful tongue. What shall be given to you, Or what shall be done to you, You false tongue? Sharp arrows of the warrior, With coals of the broom tree!" (Psalm 120:2-4).

The problem of lying is so pervasive that for centuries people have tried to come up with ways to tell if someone is actually telling the truth. In medieval English courts they had wonderful ways to detect liars, all based on the not-so-scientific notion that a person telling the truth would always be protected by God. A suspected liar would have to carry a red-hot iron bar for nine paces; either that, or he could choose to walk across nine red-hot ploughshares. Either way, if the suspected liar was burned, it was proof he was a liar, and they took him out to be hanged.

Or in some cases, the accused liar was stuffed in a sack and thrown into a pond. If the victim sank, this showed he was innocent, even though more often than not he would drown anyway. If he floated this was proof that he was lying, and he would be pulled out of the sack and hanged.

Then there's the issue of torture, which works on the assumption that if you cause people enough pain, they'll tell you the truth just to get you to stop. What's been discovered, however, is that people will tell you anything to get you to stop—whether or not it's the truth.

Centuries ago, a town in India realized that a thief lurked in their midst, so a wise man came up with a ploy to catch the thief. He put a donkey in a dark tent and told everyone that it had magical powers. If a guilty man pulled the donkey's tail, it would sing. Everyone in the village had to go into the tent alone, and pull the tail, the idea being that sooner or later the donkey would sing and the thief would be uncovered. Well, everyone lined up, and one by one they went into the tent to pull the donkey's tail. But by the time they were done, the donkey had not sung. Still, they caught the thief. How? The wise man had covered the donkey's tail with the soot from a lamp—and only one man's hands were clean at the end of the day.

Today we have polygraph tests, and we use them quite a bit even though they're notoriously inaccurate. CIA turncoat Aldrich Ames actually passed his lie detector test, even though we now know he was selling secrets to the Russians. An $860,000 government study on ten thousand hypothetical employees that included ten spies revealed that even if the polygraph did better than it usually does out in the field, two of the spies would go undetected and 1,598 innocents would be falsely accused!

Which is why we're still looking for something better. Some people think we have it in the Siemens Magnetom Trio at the University of Pennsylvania. It's basically an MRI like the ones at a hospital, but it's been designed as the world's most powerful lie detector. Supposedly, if you tell a lie the screen will light up because certain parts of your brain have been activated. How well it actually works, I don't know, but if it's true, it might be the ultimate truth detector. This certainly is a demonstration of how serious we are in investing in the project of stopping the problem of lying.

But does that mean that all lies are bad? What if you tell a lie to save someone's life? I know that some situations are difficult, but we have to be very careful, because the human brain is incredibly good at finding a justification for just about anything. The safest course of action, according to the commandment, is to be truthful. God didn't just give us this commandment because He was trying to protect the victims of lying; it's actually good for the would-be liars, as well.

At the beginning of this chapter we mentioned presidents who lied. We all know the fable about George Washington, who was asked as a child if he cut down his father's cherry tree. According to the story, he admitted it saying, "I cannot tell a lie." In response to this story, Mark Twain once said: "I am different from Washington. I have a higher and grander standard of principle. Washington could not lie. I can lie but I won't."

Let's do a hypothetical experiment. Let's assume God had made us so that we, as George Washington stated, couldn't tell a lie. I mean, suppose you were programmed in a way that it was impossible for you to lie. Think about how many other bad things you wouldn't do because you knew you couldn't lie about them. Frank isn't going to be cheating on Sally if he can't lie about where he's been, can he? Is Jones going to be pilfering the company cash register if he can't deny it in the investigation? Is Louie going to be planning the murder of Joey if Louie can't lie about where he was the night of the shooting? Take away the possibility of lying, and you change the world.

The commandment against lying is a kind of first line of defense. If we surrender our lives to God at this level, if we are determined by God's grace not to lie, then we will not allow ourselves to get into the kinds of things that all but guarantee we're going to *have* to lie. The command against lying is a defense that, if obeyed, will impact what we do in our bodies—period. The Bible says:

Your tongue devises destruction, Like a sharp razor, working deceitfully. You love evil more than good, Lying rather than speaking righteousness. Selah. You love all devouring words, You deceitful tongue. (Psalm 52:2-4)

On the other hand, if we are determined not to have a "deceitful tongue," if we are determined to obey this commandment, it's going to change our whole pattern of behavior. Think how much more at peace, how much more at ease, you would be if you didn't put yourself in situations where you felt as if you had to lie.

I suppose that to some degree everyone one of us could be named in the book, *Lies and the Lying Liars Who Tell Them,* because really, who hasn't lied? But remember what I read earlier. Jesus called the devil the "father of lies," so when we lie it's pretty serious stuff. It gives us a heritage I'm not sure we'd be proud of on the day that Jesus comes.

Deep down inside, most of us want to live in a truth-filled world. It would be good to open a financial report and know it contains absolute facts. It would be nice to listen to the editorials on news stations, and be sure that the truth is being told. It would be great if our family members and friends were always honest with us. But even though you can't make the whole world honest, there is something you can do about it. You can start with yourself.

The good news is that Jesus died for all sinners, including liars. In fact, along with your other sins, your lies nailed Him to the cross, because lying is just as sinful as breaking any one of the other commandments, even though we might be tempted to think or feel it is less sinful.

Lying is just not something we will find in the kingdom of heaven. Then why in the world would we want to do it now?

Today, right now, you can go to Jesus and confess the lies you've told and ask Him for a clean slate. You can have a fresh start with God and come clean with the people you have wronged. It's true that you might have to live with the consequences of your lies, but there's something about a clean conscience that lets you sleep a whole lot better at night. That's because now you're living the way God suggested you live in the first place—the way He designed you to live—in harmony with His law. When you love God's law, you won't feel the need to lie, in fact you will hate it.

I hate and abhor lying, But I love Your law. (Psalm 119:163)

Your problems might not disappear when you start telling the truth, but your guilty conscience will, and that's worth something; it really is. You don't have to lie to survive in this world, you honestly don't.

Living a right life can start for you right now. Take and pack the lies you've told—the burden of your sinful past to the cross of Christ and leave it with Him.

"Come to Me, all you who labor and are heavy laden, and I will give you rest. Take My yoke upon you and learn from Me, for I am gentle and lowly in heart, and you will find rest for your souls. For My yoke is easy and My burden is light." (Matthew 11:28-30)

The Bible promises, in no uncertain terms, that if we take the stains of the past—the stupid things we've done, and the lies we told to cover them up—God promises to forgive us and cleanse us. "If we confess our sins, He is faithful and just to forgive us our sins and to cleanse us from all unrighteousness" (1 John 1:9).

It's an ironclad guarantee. I know that, because God never lies.

CHAPTER ELEVEN

Nipping the Bud IN THE BUD

A friend recently told me about a remarkable trick that utterly astounded him. He was on a website where four cards from a regular deck of playing cards were taken and showed on the screen. Just four cards at random. Then he was told to fix just one of the cards in his mind. He was not to click the mouse, press a key, or touch the card in any way. He was simply to *think* about one of the cards. Let's say that, out of the four cards, he picked the king of diamonds. After he had selected the card and it was fixed in his mind, the site told him to click a button. That's it. All the cards disappeared—but then they came back, with the exception of the card he was thinking of. The king of diamonds was gone!

That kind of spooked him. There was no way a computer could possible know which card he was thinking about. So he tried it again with four different cards. This time he stepped away from the computer, way back across the room, as if putting a little more distance between him and that computer would keep it from reading his mind. He picked another card, quickly ran up to the computer and clicked on the button, then ran away again so that the computer couldn't get him. What do you think happened this time? All four cards disappeared, and when three cards reappeared, again the very card he was thinking of was missing.

My friend is a rational guy, raised and educated in the secular and scientific traditions of the world. He's also a man of faith, but his default way of thinking is usually, "There's got to be a natural explanation for this," because usually, there is. But when it came to the computer card trick, it utterly baffled him. How in the world could the computer read his mind?

He tried it a few more times and sure enough, every single time, the card he chose did not reappear on the computer screen—which tempted him to think, "Is there something supernatural going on?" Again, this is a rational person I'm talking about, someone who understands and respects the premises of natural law. At the same time, he understands something about spiritual realities, too. He's a Christian who believes in the supernatural. So the question was, "Is this computer trick something cultic? Demonic?" He didn't think so, but he wasn't sure. How in the world does a computer figure out which card he's thinking of?

It began to drive him nuts. He went downstairs and told his friend Steve what was going on. "Steve," he said, "I just can't believe what I'm seeing! How in the world can my computer know which card I'm thinking about. It's like it's reading my mind!" He expected Steve to be a little incredulous, to say something like, "That's impossible," or "Are you sure that's what's going on?" But instead Steve looked up at him and said, "You mean you don't know how that works?"

"No, I don't!"

"All they do," said Steve, "is bring back three completely different cards from the four that were originally there. You're so busy concentrating on the one you picked, you don't even notice that none of the original four came back." That was it: mystery solved. As much my friend felt like a fool for being duped by something so simple, he was actually very relieved to know that nobody was reading his mind! His experience raises a pretty good point about the sanctity of what goes on between your earlobes. I mean, let's face it; no matter how open you might be, no matter how spontaneous you are, no matter how much you might show people your feelings and emotions, we all have thoughts that are buried deep inside our minds—things that only *we* know about, and really don't want anyone else to know.

So when something comes along like this Internet card trick, and it seems like someone, or something is able to read your mind, to get inside of your most intimate space, it's a bit frightening. You've got to admit, it would be a whole lot worse than having someone read your diary. It's bad enough that our body language gives so much away (it's been said that your body language says more about what you're thinking than your actual words do), but if somebody could read your mind? That would be pretty scary.

Maybe you remember the famous novel written by George Orwell in 1948, right after World War II, called *1984.* It was his vision of the future; where every move you made was carefully monitored by the state, an institution known as BIG BROTHER. I'm not talking about being videotaped walking into a bank or a convenience store, or as you zoom past a red light. In Orwell's fantasy he is talking about someone, a live person, watching your every move—even when in your own home. In fact, in the book it gets even worse than that, because people were under the scrutiny of what was called the Thought Police, and their job was to punish wrong thoughts!

In one scene George Orwell wrote about a character:

Whether he wrote DOWN WITH BIG BROTHER, or whether he refrained from writing it, made no difference. Whether he went on with the diary, or whether he did not go on with it, made no difference. The Thought Police would get him just the same. He had committed—would still have committed, even if he had never set pen to paper—the essential crime that contained all others in itself. Thoughtcrime, they called it. Thoughtcrime was not a thing that could be concealed forever. You might dodge successfully for a while, even for years, but sooner or later they were bound to get you.

"Nothing was your own," Orwell wrote, "except the few cubic centimeters inside your own skull."

Fortunately, Orwell's nightmare fantasy for 1984—now more than two decades after the fact—turned out to be nothing *but* a fantasy. And fortunately, there's still no such thing as a computer that can read your mind.

At the same time, the Bible teaches that God knows and cares about our thoughts. But there's a significant difference: He's not doing it because He's looking for an opportunity to punish us like Orwell's Thought Police. No, on the contrary God cares about our thoughts because He wants to protect us from the kinds of things that are going to, sooner or later, bring heartache and sorrow, not just to ourselves, but also to the people around us. I guess the bottom line is this: if we can surrender even our thoughts to God, and stop thinking about wrong things, then we stand a pretty good chance of not doing those things.

We've been bombarded with secularism and atheism in the Western world. The message that seems to come through is that there really isn't any such thing as right and wrong, only what's right and wrong for you. Notice this statement from one of the world's most popular atheists, Richard Dawkins:

The universe we observe today has precisely the properties we should expect if there is at the bottom no design, no purpose, no evil, and no good, nothing but pointless indifference.

Think about that. No evil and no good? This is a brilliant man—a scholar, a writer and lecturer, and he's saying that at the core of the universe, there are no concepts of good and evil? I know that if you probe Mr. Dawkins a little more deeply, he's not going to say that things like the Rwandan Genocide or the Holocaust aren't actually evil—because I've read what he writes, and he does believe that they are. He simply thinks we developed a sense of morality all by ourselves. He's saying that right and wrong don't exist apart from us.

That sentiment comes from not believing in a higher moral power, i.e. God. You see, if God doesn't exist, then the only place we can say we get our moral values is from ourselves. If that's true, then who gets to decide what is right and wrong, or evil or good? We all have different views, depending on our backgrounds, our culture, our preferences, and our education. What one person calls evil, another person calls good. There's really no place you can build a solid foundation for everybody.

To say that evil and good don't exist outside of ourselves isn't very convincing when you actually think about it. I somehow doubt that the parents of twelve-year-old Polly Klaas, who was kidnapped and murdered in 1993, would be too impressed by all the postmodern arguments about moral relativity. And very few people really believe that "might makes right." But if we don't have a higher authority that sets the bar for us, to tell us what's right, then why not? Maybe might really *does* make right.

Instinctively we know something is wrong with that statement. Good and evil really do exist, just like the law of gravity. You find them outlined in the Ten Commandment law of God.

Now for the tenth commandment:

"You shall not covet your neighbor's house; you shall not covet your neighbor's wife, nor his male servant, nor his female servant, nor his ox, nor his donkey, nor anything that is your neighbor's." (Exodus 20:17)

This commandment takes morality to a whole new level, to the level of our thoughts. You see, if you can control what's in your head, controlling your mouth and the rest of your body should be comparatively easy. It's about nipping the bud—in the bud!

I once read about a rabbi who would summarize the Ten Commandments in the shortest phrases possible. He summarized this one as, "You shall not covet." Then he realized that wasn't quite right. That's not exactly what the commandment says.

In reality, the Bible tells me that God created us with passions and desires. He created the world full of things to delight and dazzle our senses, and He gave us the ability to enjoy those things. So technically it's not wrong to have desires. The problem comes from the *objects* of your desire, not the desire itself.

Basically, God is looking to protect us from envy, that horrible feeling you get—the one that eats you alive, dominates you—when you know that someone has more than you do, or has something you want. I'm going to presume I don't really have to describe it much, because you've probably been there, and you know what I'm talking about.

Joe lived in a town house. One day he brought home a shiny new red car. Nothing fancy, nothing ostentatious, just a shiny new red car to get himself back and forth to work. But the next day Joe's next-door neighbor came home with a bigger, nicer, and fancier shiny new red car. It was almost like the neighbor had been jealous of Joe. I'll bet you can guess what happened. Joe started feeling just a little jealous himself. Then a couple of days later, two doors down, another neighbor bought an even bigger and shinier red car than the both of them!

I know we smile about it, but that's because we've been there, and the problem is as old as the human race. Lycurgus was the father of the ancient kingdom of Sparta. He became so concerned about the economic envy and jealousy between the different classes in Sparta, that he created a new economy. He ordered that all the gold and silver had to be turned in, and cheap iron be used for money instead. Because it was so cheap and common, people needed carts and oxen to carry their money around with them. Suddenly, buying and selling became a huge burden, and a whole host of evils all but disappeared. Who was going to rob someone if they couldn't hide their theft? And who was going to take a bribe if they couldn't hide their ill-gotten gain? A great deal of luxury and ostentatious living was curtailed because it just became too difficult to buy things. All of a sudden people were more content with owning the little bit they did have.

Maybe you've heard the story of the man who was given a special gift: Whatever he wanted, whatever he wished for, would be his. There was only one small catch; no matter what he got, his neighbor got double.

The man wished for a big estate, a big farm with land and servants, and he got it. But then his neighbor got an estate and farm twice as big, with twice as many servants. He wanted a beautiful new carriage, and he got it. But then his neighbor got two beautiful new carriages. He wanted a stable full of racing horses, and he got it. But then his neighbor got a stable twice the size, with twice as many horses.

On and on it went. No matter what he got, he was consumed with envy, because his neighbor got twice as much. Finally, unable to stand it any more, unable to enjoy his own newfound riches, he wished he could be blind in one eye!

Let's be honest about this. Think about how much better our lives would be were we to take this tenth commandment to heart. In many ways this might be the hardest commandment of all to actually keep. Most folks don't have a problem not committing murder, or theft, or adultery or idolatry; but not being jealous when someone has more than you? That's not quite so easy. You don't have to sneak around at night or lurk in back alleys with sunglasses to do it. It's a sin that you can commit in broad daylight in a room full of people, and nobody will know it—except for God.

Let me give you a biblical principle from the writings of Paul that is very helpful:

Not that I speak in regard to need, for I have learned in whatever state I am, to be content: I know how to be abased, and I know how to abound. Everywhere and in all things I have learned both to be full and to be hungry, both to abound and to suffer need. I can do all things through Christ who strengthens me. (Philippians 4:11-13)

Here's another one from Paul:

Let your conduct be without covetousness; be content with such things as you have. For He Himself has said, "I will never leave you nor forsake you." (Hebrews 13:5)

No matter who you are, you're going to have more than somebody else. And I promise you, somebody else is going to have more than you. That's just the way it is. So how are you supposed to deal with it? By being content; by being thankful for what you do have.

There are stories going around about multi-billionaire Larry Ellison being envious of Bill Gates, because Gates is richer than he is. If that's true, and I don't know for sure that it is, Mr. Ellison might feel a whole lot better if he focused on all the poor multi-millionaires who have less than he does!

In ancient Rome, some ambassadors from another country came to try and bribe Dentatus, who was the counsel of Rome. They found him living in some small unpretentious cottage. As they approached they saw that he was making lunch. He was boiling a few turnips and that was all. They knew right then that theirs was a lost cause. It was obvious that money wasn't going to do the trick, because how in the world do you bribe somebody who is happy with turnips?

A certain couple had been living in the same home for years. But suddenly, very dissatisfied with their house and wanting something more, they asked an agent to sell it while they looked for another one. One day as they scanned the ads, they read about a house that seemed like the home of their dreams.

"Let's go see it!" they said, all excited about the prospects of their new dream house. As it turned out, they were reading the ad their agent had put in the paper for their own home! If we were to count our blessings, and look at our situation as someone else might, it would be amazing how often we'd be happy with just what we have.

Who hasn't struggled with this sin? (And it is a sin, because God lists it in the Ten Commandments, and He tells us that sin is the transgression of God's law.) To some degree or other, we've all broken this tenth and final commandment. So what are we to do?

The answer is remarkably simple: You go to Jesus who died so that we can be forgiven, not just for coveting, but for everything: all our wrong thoughts, and all our wrong actions. Think of all the evil, the suffering, the pain in our world caused by greed and jealousy. That's why God gave us this commandment: to nip covetousness in the bud before it grows into its deadly fruit. Jesus can free us from the tyranny of jealousy. He knows that it will eat you alive if you don't get your feelings under control. So He offers to free us from it, if we let Him.

Someone once said that a key to living a good life is to dwell on Jesus, on His life, His character, His deeds, His selflessness, His goodness, His willingness to forgive. The idea is that by doing this, we will become more like Him. And that's a gift we really shouldn't refuse. In fact, to be like Jesus is something you *should* covet, and God won't mind a bit. In fact, the Bible encourages us to copy Jesus.

Let this mind be in you which was also in Christ Jesus. (Philippians 2:5)

So why not turn to the One who has never broken one of God's commandments and aim to model your life after His? After all, He came to *live* the law and died not to do away with the law but to fulfill it.

"Do not think that I came to destroy the Law or the Prophets. I did not come to destroy but to fulfill. For assuredly, I say to you, till heaven and earth pass away, one jot or one tittle will by no means pass from the law till all is fulfilled." (Matthew 5:17, 18)

Jesus came to show that God's law is a law of love. He demonstrated just exactly how far that kind of love was willing to go. That Love in the most extreme sense was willing to die for you.

"Greater love has no one than this, than to lay down one's life for his friends." (John 15:13)

Jesus came to show us that our God is a God of love and forgiveness, not a God who is looking to condemn us. God is in the business of saving people!

"For God did not send His Son into the world to condemn the world, but that the world through Him might be saved." (John 3:17)

Jesus wants to save you from your sin and help you live a life of love. He said that love is what the law is all about—that the law can be summed up in loving God and loving those around us. Living according to the Ten Commandments means living a life of love.

"And you shall love the LORD your God with all your heart, with all your soul, with all your mind, and with all your strength. This is the first commandment. And the second, like it, is this: You shall love your neighbor as yourself. There is no other commandment greater than these." (Mark 12:30, 31)

The Ten Commandments written on tables of stone were given to us for our good. They were designed to bless our lives with love, joy and peace. These moral principles protect us from the evil that surrounds us in this world of sin. They form the foundation of eternal security for the entire universe. And they show that God is love. Why not open your life to experience that kind of love today? You'll discover that living according to God's plan is a much better way to live.

Discover Answers to life's Questions

Bibleinfo.com

offers answers to hundreds of everyday questions. Discover what the Bible has to say about your question. The answer is only a click away!

Kids**Bible**info.com™

big answers for little people℠

Plus, there is a fun, educational and inspirational site designed for children. Explore interactive games, Bible lessons, character-building stories and more at www.KidsBibleinfo.com.

Bibleinfo.com®

Bible answers to hundreds of life's questions in 18 languages.